MznLnx

Missing Links Exam Preps

Exam Prep for

Core Concepts of Operations Management

Vonderembse & White, 1st Edition

The MznLnx Exam Prep is your link from the texbook and lecture to your exams.
The MznLnx Exam Preps are unauthorized and comprehensive reviews of your textbooks.

All material provided by MznLnx and Rico Publications (c) 2010
Textbook publishers and textbook authors do not particpate in or contribute to these reviews.

MznLnx

Rico Publications

Exam Prep for Core Concepts of Operations Management
1st Edition
Vonderembse & White

Publisher: Raymond Houge
Assistant Editor: Michael Rouger
Text and Cover Designer: Lisa Buckner
Marketing Manager: Sara Swagger
Project Manager, Editorial Production: Jerry Emerson
Art Director: Vernon Lowerui

Product Manager: Dave Mason
Editorial Assitant: Rachel Guzmanji
Pedagogy: Debra Long
Cover Image: Jim Reed/Getty Images
Text and Cover Printer: City Printing, Inc.
Compositor: Media Mix, Inc.

(c) 2010 Rico Publications

ALL RIGHTS RESERVED. No part of this work covered by the copyright may be reproduced or used in any form or by an means--graphic, electronic, or mechanical, including photocopying, recording, taping, Web distribution, information storage, and retrieval systems, or in any other manner--without the written permission of the publisher.

Printed in the United States
ISBN:

For more information about our products, contact us at:
Dave.Mason@RicoPublications.com

For permission to use material from this text or product, submit a request online to:
Dave.Mason@RicoPublications.com

Contents

CHAPTER 1
Introduction to Operations Management in a Global Environment   1

CHAPTER 2
Gaining Competitive Advantage Through Operations   9

CHAPTER 3
Enhancing Productivity: A Key to Sccess   19

CHAPTER 4
Quality Management   26

CHAPTER 5
Enterprise Integration and Supply Chain Management: A Strategic Perspective   34

CHAPTER 6
Product Development: A Team Approach   46

CHAPTER 7
Models and Forecasting   52

CHAPTER 8
Process Selection: Volume Drives Costs and Profits   60

CHAPTER 9
Capacity Decisions   67

CHAPTER 10
Facility Location in a Global Environment   73

CHAPTER 11
Facility Layout   77

CHAPTER 12
Aggregate Planning   85

CHAPTER 13
Planning for Material and Resource Requirements   91

CHAPTER 14
Inventory Management   98

CHAPTER 15
Just-in-Time and Theory of Constraints   103

CHAPTER 16
Scheduling   110

CHAPTER 17
Project Management   117

ANSWER KEY   121

TO THE STUDENT

COMPREHENSIVE

The *MznLnx* Exam Prep series is designed to help you pass your exams. Editors at MznLnx review your textbooks and then prepare these practice exams to help you master the textbook material. Unlike study guides, workbooks, and practice tests provided by the texbook publisher and textbook authors, *MznLnx* gives you **all** of the material in each chapter in exam form, not just samples, so you can be sure to nail your exam.

MECHANICAL

The MznLnx Exam Prep series creates exams that will help you learn the subject matter as well as test you on your understanding. Each question is designed to help you master the concept. Just working through the exams, you gain an understanding of the subject--its a simple mechanical process that produces success.

INTEGRATED STUDY GUIDE AND REVIEW

MznLnx is not just a set of exams designed to test you, its also a comprehensive review of the subject content. Each exam question is also a review of the concept, making sure that you will get the answer correct without having to go to other sources of material. You learn as you go! Its the easiest way to pass an exam.

HUMOR

Studying can be tedious and dry. MznLnx's instructional design includes moderate humor within the exam questions on occassion, to break the tedium and revitalize the brain

Chapter 1. Introduction to Operations Management in a Global Environment

1. The _____ is a trilateral trade bloc in North America created by the governments of the United States, Canada, and Mexico. The agreement creating the trade bloc came into force on January 1, 1994. It superseded the Canada-United States Free Trade Agreement between the U.S. and Canada.
   a. Career portfolios
   b. Trade union
   c. Business war game
   d. North American Free Trade Agreement

2. _____ are statistical methods developed by Genichi Taguchi to improve the quality of manufactured goods, and more recently also applied to biotechnology, marketing and advertising. Professional statisticians have welcomed the goals and improvements brought about by _____, particularly by Taguchi's development of designs for studying variation, but have criticized the inefficiency of some of Taguchi's proposals.

Taguchi's work includes three principal contributions to statistics:

   1. Taguchi loss function;
   2. The philosophy of off-line quality control; and
   3. Innovations in the design of experiments.

Traditionally, statistical methods have relied on mean-unbiased estimators of treatment effects: Under the conditions of the Gauss-Markov theorem, least squares estimators have minimum variance among all mean-unbiased estimators. The emphasis on comparisons of means also draws (limiting) comfort from the law of large numbers, according to which the sample means converge to the true mean.

   a. Taguchi methods
   b. Design of experiments
   c. 28-hour day
   d. 1990 Clean Air Act

3. _____ concern the operation of a facility, as opposed to maintenance, supply and distribution, health, and safety, emergency response, human resources, security, information technology and other infrastructural support organizations.

Personnel that make up 'operations' are

   - operators
   - engineers
   - technicians
   - management

This is mainly in a manufacturing setting.

Chapter 1. Introduction to Operations Management in a Global Environment

a. Conglomerate merger
b. Labor intensive
c. Manufacturing operations
d. Market niche

4. _____ is an advertisement in which a particular product specifically mentions a competitor by name for the express purpose of showing why the competitor is inferior to the product naming it.

This should not be confused with parody advertisements, where a fictional product is being advertised for the purpose of poking fun at the particular advertisement, nor should it be confused with the use of a coined brand name for the purpose of comparing the product without actually naming an actual competitor. ('Wikipedia tastes better and is less filling than the Encyclopedia Galactica.')

In the 1980s, during what has been referred to as the cola wars, soft-drink manufacturer Pepsi ran a series of advertisements where people, caught on hidden camera, in a blind taste test, chose Pepsi over rival Coca-Cola.

a. 1990 Clean Air Act
b. 28-hour day
c. Comparative advertising
d. 33 Strategies of War

5. _____ is an area of business concerned with the production of goods and services, and involves the responsibility of ensuring that business operations are efficient in terms of using as little resource as needed, and effective in terms of meeting customer requirements. It is concerned with managing the process that converts inputs (in the forms of materials, labour and energy) into outputs (in the form of goods and services.)

Operations traditionally refers to the production of goods and services separately, although the distinction between these two main types of operations is increasingly difficult to make as manufacturers tend to merge product and service offerings.

a. AAAI
b. A Stake in the Outcome
c. A4e
d. Operations management

6. _____ ('Plan-Do-Check-Act') is an iterative four-step problem-solving process typically used in business process improvement. It is also known as the Deming Cycle, Shewhart cycle, Deming Wheel, or Plan-Do-Study-Act.

_____ was made popular by Dr. W. Edwards Deming, who is considered by many to be the father of modern quality control; however it was always referred to by him as the Shewhart cycle. Later in Deming's career, he modified _____ to Plan, Do, Study, Act (PDSA) so as to better describe his recommendations.

a. Management by exception
b. Decentralization
c. Management team
d. PDCA

7. _____ refers to the difference between the cost of materials purchased by a company plus the cost of the labor to assemble a product and the price at which the company sells the product. An example is the price of gasoline at the pump over the price of the oil in it. In national accounts used in macroeconomics, it refers to the contribution of the factors of production, i.e., land, labor, and capital goods, to raising the value of a product and corresponds to the incomes received by the owners of these factors.
a. Rehn-Meidner Model
b. Minimum wage
c. Value added
d. Deregulation

8. Procter is a surname, and may also refer to:

- Bryan Waller Procter (pseud. Barry Cornwall), English poet
- Goodwin Procter, American law firm
- _____, consumer products multinational

a. Strict liability
b. Procter ' Gamble
c. Downstream
d. Master and Servant Acts

9. _____ is used for the design, development, analysis, and optimization of technical processes and is mainly applied to chemical plants and chemical processes, but also to power stations, and similar technical facilities. Process flow diagram of a typical amine treating process used in industrial plants

_____ is a model-based representation of chemical, physical, biological, and other technical processes and unit operations in software. Basic prerequisites are a thorough knowledge of chemical and physical properties of pure components and mixtures, of reactions, and of mathematical models which, in combination, allow the calculation of a process in computers.

a. 1990 Clean Air Act
b. 33 Strategies of War
c. Process simulation
d. 28-hour day

10. _____ can be defined as the idea generation, concept development, testing and manufacturing or implementation of a physical object or service. _____ers conceptualize and evaluate ideas, making them tangible through products in a more systematic approach. The role of a _____er encompasses many characteristics of the marketing manager, product manager, industrial designer and design engineer.
   a. Adam Smith
   b. Abraham Harold Maslow
   c. Affiliation
   d. Product design

11. The _____ is the labour pool in employment. It is generally used to describe those working for a single company or industry, but can also apply to a geographic region like a city, country, state, etc. The term generally excludes the employers or management, and implies those involved in manual labour.
   a. Pink-collar worker
   b. Work-life balance
   c. Division of labour
   d. Workforce

12. _____ is a work methodology based on the parallelization of tasks (ie. concurrently.) It refers to an approach used in product development in which functions of design engineering, manufacturing engineering and other functions are integrated to reduce the elapsed time required to bring a new product to the market.
   a. Project management
   b. Critical Chain Project Management
   c. Concurrent engineering
   d. Work package

13. _____ refers to increasing the spiritual, political, social or economic strength of individuals and communities. It often involves the empowered developing confidence in their own capacities.

The term Human _____ covers a vast landscape of meanings, interpretations, definitions and disciplines ranging from psychology and philosophy to the highly commercialized Self-Help industry and Motivational sciences.

a. AAAI
b. A Stake in the Outcome
c. Empowerment
d. A4e

14. The field of _____ looks at the relationship between management and workers, particularly groups of workers represented by a union.

_____ is an important factor in analyzing 'varieties of capitalism', such as neocorporatism, social democracy, and neoliberalism

a. Informal organization
b. Industrial relations
c. Organizational effectiveness
d. Overtime

15. The _____, widely known as ISO , is an international-standard-setting body composed of representatives from various national standards organizations. Founded on 23 February 1947, the organization promulgates worldwide proprietary industrial and commercial standards. It is headquartered in Geneva, Switzerland.
a. AAAI
b. International Organization for Standardization
c. A4e
d. A Stake in the Outcome

16. In statistics, _____ refers to techniques for the modeling and analysis of numerical data consisting of values of a dependent variable and of one or more independent variables The dependent variable in the regression equation is modeled as a function of the independent variables, corresponding parameters, and an error term. The error term is treated as a random variable and represents unexplained variation in the dependent variable.
a. Least squares
b. Regression analysis
c. Stepwise regression
d. Trend analysis

17. _____ is a strategic planning method used to evaluate the Strengths, Weaknesses, Opportunities, and Threats involved in a project or in a business venture. It involves specifying the objective of the business venture or project and identifying the internal and external factors that are favorable and unfavorable to achieving that objective. The technique is credited to Albert Humphrey, who led a convention at Stanford University in the 1960s and 1970s using data from Fortune 500 companies.

a. Market share
b. Corporate image
c. Marketing
d. SWOT analysis

18. In management science, operations research and organizational development (OD), human organizations are viewed as systems (conceptual systems) of interacting components such as _____ or system aggregates, which are carriers of numerous complex processes and organizational structures. Organizational development theorist Peter Senge developed the notion of organizations as systems in his book The Fifth Discipline.

Systems thinking is a style of thinking/reasoning and problem solving.

a. 1990 Clean Air Act
b. 28-hour day
c. Systems thinking
d. Subsystems

19. An _____ is the negative aspects of human activity on the biophysical environment. Environmentalism, a social and environmental movement that started in the 1960s, focuses on addressing _____ s through advocacy, education and activism.

Major current _____ s are climate change, pollution and resource depletion.

a. Environmental issue
b. A4e
c. A Stake in the Outcome
d. AAAI

20. A _____ is a formal statement of a set of business goals, the reasons why they are believed attainable, and the plan for reaching those goals. It may also contain background information about the organization or team attempting to reach those goals.

The business goals may be defined for for-profit or for non-profit organizations.

a. Crisis management
b. Time management
c. Business plan
d. Distributed management

Chapter 1. Introduction to Operations Management in a Global Environment

21. A _____ or business method is a collection of related, structured activities or tasks that produce a specific service or product (serve a particular goal) for a particular customer or customers. It often can be visualized with a flowchart as a sequence of activities.

There are three types of _____es:

1. Management processes, the processes that govern the operation of a system. Typical management processes include 'Corporate Governance' and 'Strategic Management'.
2. Operational processes, processes that constitute the core business and create the primary value stream. Typical operational processes are Purchasing, Manufacturing, Marketing, and Sales.
3. Supporting processes, which support the core processes. Examples include Accounting, Recruitment, Technical support.

A _____ begins with a customer's need and ends with a customer's need fulfillment. Process oriented organizations break down the barriers of structural departments and try to avoid functional silos.

a. 28-hour day
b. 33 Strategies of War
c. 1990 Clean Air Act
d. Business process

22. _____ is an integrated communications-based process through which individuals and communities discover that existing and newly-identified needs and wants may be satisfied by the products and services of others.

_____ is defined by the American _____ Association as the activity, set of institutions, and processes for creating, communicating, delivering, and exchanging offerings that have value for customers, clients, partners, and society at large. The term developed from the original meaning which referred literally to going to market, as in shopping, or going to a market to buy or sell goods or services.

a. Marketing
b. Disruptive technology
c. Market development
d. Customer relationship management

23. An _____ is a mostly hierarchical concept of subordination of entities that collaborate and contribute to serve one common aim.

Organizations are a variant of clustered entities. The structure of an organization is usually set up in many a styles, dependent on their objectives and ambience.

a. Organizational development
b. Informal organization
c. Open shop
d. Organizational structure

24. Marketing research is a form of business research and is generally divided into two categories: consumer _____ and business-to-business (B2B) _____, which was previously known as industrial marketing research. Consumer marketing research studies the buying habits of individual people while business-to-business marketing research investigates the markets for products sold by one business to another.

Consumer _____ is a form of applied sociology that concentrates on understanding the behaviours, whims and preferences, of consumers in a market-based economy, and aims to understand the effects and comparative success of marketing campaigns.

a. Questionnaire
b. Questionnaire construction
c. Mystery shoppers
d. Market research

Chapter 2. Gaining Competitive Advantage Through Operations

1. _____ is, in very basic words, a position a firm occupies against its competitors.

According to Michael Porter, the three methods for creating a sustainable _____ are through:

1. Cost leadership

2. Differentiation

3. Focus (economics)

   a. 28-hour day
   b. Theory Z
   c. 1990 Clean Air Act
   d. Competitive advantage

2. _____, in strategic management and marketing is, according to Carlton O'Neal, the percentage or proportion of the total available market or market segment that is being serviced by a company. It can be expressed as a company's sales revenue (from that market) divided by the total sales revenue available in that market. It can also be expressed as a company's unit sales volume (in a market) divided by the total volume of units sold in that market.
   a. Green marketing
   b. Marketing plan
   c. Business-to-business
   d. Market share

3. _____ is a strategic planning method used to evaluate the Strengths, Weaknesses, Opportunities, and Threats involved in a project or in a business venture. It involves specifying the objective of the business venture or project and identifying the internal and external factors that are favorable and unfavorable to achieving that objective. The technique is credited to Albert Humphrey, who led a convention at Stanford University in the 1960s and 1970s using data from Fortune 500 companies.
   a. SWOT analysis
   b. Marketing
   c. Market share
   d. Corporate image

4. A _____ or business method is a collection of related, structured activities or tasks that produce a specific service or product (serve a particular goal) for a particular customer or customers. It often can be visualized with a flowchart as a sequence of activities.

There are three types of _____es:

1. Management processes, the processes that govern the operation of a system. Typical management processes include 'Corporate Governance' and 'Strategic Management'.
2. Operational processes, processes that constitute the core business and create the primary value stream. Typical operational processes are Purchasing, Manufacturing, Marketing, and Sales.
3. Supporting processes, which support the core processes. Examples include Accounting, Recruitment, Technical support.

A _____ begins with a customer's need and ends with a customer's need fulfillment. Process oriented organizations break down the barriers of structural departments and try to avoid functional silos.

a. 33 Strategies of War
b. 28-hour day
c. 1990 Clean Air Act
d. Business process

5. The _____, widely known as ISO , is an international-standard-setting body composed of representatives from various national standards organizations. Founded on 23 February 1947, the organization promulgates worldwide proprietary industrial and commercial standards. It is headquartered in Geneva, Switzerland.
a. A Stake in the Outcome
b. International Organization for Standardization
c. AAAI
d. A4e

6. Procter is a surname, and may also refer to:

- Bryan Waller Procter (pseud. Barry Cornwall), English poet
- Goodwin Procter, American law firm
- _____, consumer products multinational

a. Master and Servant Acts
b. Strict liability
c. Downstream
d. Procter ' Gamble

Chapter 2. Gaining Competitive Advantage Through Operations

7. _____ refers to metrics and measures of output from production processes, per unit of input. Labor _____, for example, is typically measured as a ratio of output per labor-hour, an input. _____ may be conceived of as a metrics of the technical or engineering efficiency of production.

   a. Productivity
   b. Remanufacturing
   c. Value engineering
   d. Master production schedule

8. In statistics, _____ refers to techniques for the modeling and analysis of numerical data consisting of values of a dependent variable and of one or more independent variables The dependent variable in the regression equation is modeled as a function of the independent variables, corresponding parameters, and an error term. The error term is treated as a random variable and represents unexplained variation in the dependent variable.

   a. Trend analysis
   b. Least squares
   c. Stepwise regression
   d. Regression analysis

9. _____ are statistical methods developed by Genichi Taguchi to improve the quality of manufactured goods, and more recently also applied to biotechnology, marketing and advertising. Professional statisticians have welcomed the goals and improvements brought about by _____, particularly by Taguchi's development of designs for studying variation, but have criticized the inefficiency of some of Taguchi's proposals.

Taguchi's work includes three principal contributions to statistics:

   1. Taguchi loss function;
   2. The philosophy of off-line quality control; and
   3. Innovations in the design of experiments.

Traditionally, statistical methods have relied on mean-unbiased estimators of treatment effects: Under the conditions of the Gauss-Markov theorem, least squares estimators have minimum variance among all mean-unbiased estimators. The emphasis on comparisons of means also draws (limiting) comfort from the law of large numbers, according to which the sample means converge to the true mean.

   a. 1990 Clean Air Act
   b. Taguchi methods
   c. 28-hour day
   d. Design of experiments

Chapter 2. Gaining Competitive Advantage Through Operations

10. In economics, business, retail, and accounting, a _____ is the value of money that has been used up to produce something, and hence is not available for use anymore. In economics, a _____ is an alternative that is given up as a result of a decision. In business, the _____ may be one of acquisition, in which case the amount of money expended to acquire it is counted as _____.

   a. Cost allocation
   b. Cost overrun
   c. Fixed costs
   d. Cost

11. _____ describes commerce transactions between businesses, such as between a manufacturer and a wholesaler, or between a wholesaler and a retailer. Contrasting terms are business-to-consumer (B2C) and business-to-government (B2G.)

The volume of B2B transactions is much higher than the volume of B2C transactions.

   a. Market environment
   b. Product bundling
   c. Category management
   d. Business-to-business

12. Business-to-consumer describes activities of businesses serving end consumers with products and/or services.

An example of a _____ transaction would be a person buying a pair of shoes from a retailer. The transactions that led to the shoes being available for purchase, that is the purchase of the leather, laces, rubber, etc.

   a. Market environment
   b. Green marketing
   c. PEST analysis
   d. B2C

13. _____ consists of the processes a company uses to track and organize its contacts with its current and prospective customers. _____ software is used to support these processes; information about customers and customer interactions can be entered, stored and accessed by employees in different company departments. Typical _____ goals are to improve services provided to customers, and to use customer contact information for targeted marketing.

a. Marketing plan
b. Disruptive technology
c. Customer relationship management
d. Green marketing

14. _____, commonly known as e-commerce, consists of the buying and selling of products or services over electronic systems such as the Internet and other computer networks. The amount of trade conducted electronically has grown extraordinarily with widespread Internet usage. The use of commerce is conducted in this way, spurring and drawing on innovations in electronic funds transfer, supply chain management, Internet marketing, online transaction processing, electronic data interchange (EDI), inventory management systems, and automated data collection systems.
a. Online shopping
b. A Stake in the Outcome
c. A4e
d. Electronic Commerce

15. A _____ is the system of organizations, people, technology, activities, information and resources involved in moving a product or service from supplier to customer. _____ activities transform natural resources, raw materials and components into a finished product that is delivered to the end customer. In sophisticated _____ systems, used products may re-enter the _____ at any point where residual value is recyclable.
a. Drop shipping
b. Wholesalers
c. Packaging
d. Supply chain

16. _____ is the management of a network of interconnected businesses involved in the ultimate provision of product and service packages required by end customers (Harland, 1996.) _____ spans all movement and storage of raw materials, work-in-process inventory, and finished goods from point of origin to point of consumption (supply chain.)

The definition an American professional association put forward is that _____ encompasses the planning and management of all activities involved in sourcing, procurement, conversion, and logistics management activities.

a. Drop shipping
b. Packaging
c. Freight forwarder
d. Supply chain management

Chapter 2. Gaining Competitive Advantage Through Operations

17. _____ is the process of estimation in unknown situations. Prediction is a similar, but more general term. Both can refer to estimation of time series, cross-sectional or longitudinal data.
    a. 28-hour day
    b. 33 Strategies of War
    c. 1990 Clean Air Act
    d. Forecasting

18. In business and engineering, new _____ is the term used to describe the complete process of bringing a new product or service to market. There are two parallel paths involved in the NProduct development process: one involves the idea generation, product design, and detail engineering; the other involves market research and marketing analysis. Companies typically see new _____ as the first stage in generating and commercializing new products within the overall strategic process of product life cycle management used to maintain or grow their market share.
    a. 33 Strategies of War
    b. 28-hour day
    c. 1990 Clean Air Act
    d. Product development

19. _____ is an organization's process of defining its strategy and making decisions on allocating its resources to pursue this strategy, including its capital and people. Various business analysis techniques can be used in _____, including SWOT analysis (Strengths, Weaknesses, Opportunities, and Threats) and PEST analysis (Political, Economic, Social, and Technological analysis) or STEER analysis involving Socio-cultural, Technological, Economic, Ecological, and Regulatory factors and EPISTEL (Environment, Political, Informatic, Social, Technological, Economic and Legal)

_____ is the formal consideration of an organization's future course. All _____ deals with at least one of three key questions:

1. 'What do we do?'
2. 'For whom do we do it?'
3. 'How do we excel?'

In business _____, the third question is better phrased 'How can we beat or avoid competition?'. (Bradford and Duncan, page 1.)

   a. 1990 Clean Air Act
   b. 33 Strategies of War
   c. 28-hour day
   d. Strategic planning

Chapter 2. Gaining Competitive Advantage Through Operations

20. _____ is the term used to describe a situation where different entities cooperate advantageously for a final outcome. Simply defined, it means that the whole is greater than the sum of the individual parts. Although the whole will be greater than each individual part, this is not the concept of _____.
   a. 33 Strategies of War
   b. Synergy
   c. 28-hour day
   d. 1990 Clean Air Act

21. _____ refers to the overarching strategy of the diversified firm. Such a _____ answers the questions of 'in which businesses should we be in?' and 'how does being in these business create synergy and/or add to the competitive advantage of the corporation as a whole?'

Business strategy refers to the aggregated strategies of single business firm or a strategic business unit (SBU) in a diversified corporation. According to Michael Porter, a firm must formulate a business strategy that incorporates either cost leadership, differentiation or focus in order to achieve a sustainable competitive advantage and long-term success in its chosen arenas or industries.

   a. Strategic drift
   b. Competitive heterogeneity
   c. Strategic group
   d. Corporate strategy

22. The _____ is a trilateral trade bloc in North America created by the governments of the United States, Canada, and Mexico. The agreement creating the trade bloc came into force on January 1, 1994. It superseded the Canada-United States Free Trade Agreement between the U.S. and Canada.
   a. Business war game
   b. Trade union
   c. North American Free Trade Agreement
   d. Career portfolios

23. An _____ is the negative aspects of human activity on the biophysical environment. Environmentalism, a social and environmental movement that started in the 1960s, focuses on addressing _____s through advocacy, education and activism.

Major current _____s are climate change, pollution and resource depletion.

a. A4e
b. AAAI
c. A Stake in the Outcome
d. Environmental issue

24. _____ concern the operation of a facility, as opposed to maintenance, supply and distribution, health, and safety, emergency response, human resources, security, information technology and other infrastructural support organizations.

Personnel that make up 'operations' are

- operators
- engineers
- technicians
- management

This is mainly in a manufacturing setting.

a. Manufacturing operations
b. Conglomerate merger
c. Labor intensive
d. Market niche

25. _____ constitute a class of computer-based information systems including knowledge-based systems that support decision-making activities.

_____ are a specific class of computerized information systems that supports business and organizational decision-making activities. A properly-designed _____ is an interactive software-based system intended to help decision makers compile useful information from raw data, documents, personal knowledge, and/or business models to identify and solve problems and make decisions.

a. 28-hour day
b. Decision support systems
c. 1990 Clean Air Act
d. Spatial Decision Support Systems

Chapter 2. Gaining Competitive Advantage Through Operations

26. An _____ is software that attempts to reproduce the performance of one or more human experts, most commonly in a specific problem domain, and is a traditional application and/or subfield of artificial intelligence. A wide variety of methods can be used to simulate the performance of the expert however common to most or all are 1) the creation of a so-called 'knowledgebase' which uses some knowledge representation formalism to capture the Subject Matter Experts (SME) knowledge and 2) a process of gathering that knowledge from the SME and codifying it according to the formalism, which is called knowledge engineering. _____s may or may not have learning components but a third common element is that once the system is developed it is proven by being placed in the same real world problem solving situation as the human SME, typically as an aid to human workers or a supplement to some information system.

   a. A4e
   b. Expert system
   c. AAAI
   d. A Stake in the Outcome

27. _____ is an advertisement in which a particular product specifically mentions a competitor by name for the express purpose of showing why the competitor is inferior to the product naming it.

This should not be confused with parody advertisements, where a fictional product is being advertised for the purpose of poking fun at the particular advertisement, nor should it be confused with the use of a coined brand name for the purpose of comparing the product without actually naming an actual competitor. ('Wikipedia tastes better and is less filling than the Encyclopedia Galactica.')

In the 1980s, during what has been referred to as the cola wars, soft-drink manufacturer Pepsi ran a series of advertisements where people, caught on hidden camera, in a blind taste test, chose Pepsi over rival Coca-Cola.

   a. Comparative advertising
   b. 1990 Clean Air Act
   c. 33 Strategies of War
   d. 28-hour day

28. _____ is the use of control systems (such as numerical control, programmable logic control, and other industrial control systems), in concert with other applications of information technology (such as computer-aided technologies [CAD, CAM, CAx]), to control industrial machinery and processes, reducing the need for human intervention. In the scope of industrialization, _____ is a step beyond mechanization. Whereas mechanization provided human operators with machinery to assist them with the physical requirements of work, _____ greatly reduces the need for human sensory and mental requirements as well.

   a. A4e
   b. A Stake in the Outcome
   c. AAAI
   d. Automation

Chapter 2. Gaining Competitive Advantage Through Operations

29. _____ in engineering is a method of manufacturing in which the entire production process is controlled by computer. The traditional separated process methods are joined through a computer by CIM. This integration allows that the processes exchange information with each other and they are able to initiate actions.

   a. 28-hour day
   b. 33 Strategies of War
   c. Computer-integrated manufacturing
   d. 1990 Clean Air Act

30. _____ is one of the managerial functions like planning, organizing, staffing and directing. It is an important function because it helps to check the errors and to take the corrective action so that deviation from standards are minimized and stated goals of the organization are achieved in desired manner. According to modern concepts, _____ is a foreseeing action whereas earlier concept of _____ was used only when errors were detected. _____ in management means setting standards, measuring actual performance and taking corrective action.

   a. Control
   b. Schedule of reinforcement
   c. Turnover
   d. Decision tree pruning

31. A _____ system is a manufacturing system in which there is some amount of flexibility that allows the system to react in the case of changes, whether predicted or unpredicted. This flexibility is generally considered to fall into two categories, which both contain numerous subcategories.

The first category, machine flexibility, covers the system's ability to be changed to produce new product types, and ability to change the order of operations executed on a part. The second category is called routing flexibility, which consists of the ability to use multiple machines to perform the same operation on a part, as well as the system's ability to absorb large-scale changes, such as in volume, capacity, or capability.

   a. Manufacturing resource planning
   b. Homeworkers
   c. Jidoka
   d. Flexible manufacturing

Chapter 3. Enhancing Productivity: A Key to Sccess

1. _____ is a concept that aims to enhance supply chain integration by supporting and assisting joint practices. _____ seeks cooperative management of inventory through joint visibility and replenishment of products throughout the supply chain. Information shared between suppliers and retailers aids in planning and satisfying customer demands through a supportive system of shared information.
   a. Career portfolios
   b. Timesheets
   c. Groups decision making
   d. Collaborative Planning, Forecasting and Replenishment

2. Procter is a surname, and may also refer to:

   - Bryan Waller Procter (pseud. Barry Cornwall), English poet
   - Goodwin Procter, American law firm
   - _____, consumer products multinational

   a. Strict liability
   b. Procter ' Gamble
   c. Master and Servant Acts
   d. Downstream

3. _____ refers to metrics and measures of output from production processes, per unit of input. Labor _____, for example, is typically measured as a ratio of output per labor-hour, an input. _____ may be conceived of as a metrics of the technical or engineering efficiency of production.
   a. Value engineering
   b. Remanufacturing
   c. Master production schedule
   d. Productivity

4. _____ are statistical methods developed by Genichi Taguchi to improve the quality of manufactured goods, and more recently also applied to biotechnology, marketing and advertising. Professional statisticians have welcomed the goals and improvements brought about by _____, particularly by Taguchi's development of designs for studying variation, but have criticized the inefficiency of some of Taguchi's proposals.

Taguchi's work includes three principal contributions to statistics:

   1. Taguchi loss function;
   2. The philosophy of off-line quality control; and
   3. Innovations in the design of experiments.

Traditionally, statistical methods have relied on mean-unbiased estimators of treatment effects: Under the conditions of the Gauss-Markov theorem, least squares estimators have minimum variance among all mean-unbiased estimators. The emphasis on comparisons of means also draws (limiting) comfort from the law of large numbers, according to which the sample means converge to the true mean.

a. 28-hour day
b. Taguchi methods
c. 1990 Clean Air Act
d. Design of experiments

5. _____ is the use of control systems (such as numerical control, programmable logic control, and other industrial control systems), in concert with other applications of information technology (such as computer-aided technologies [CAD, CAM, CAx]), to control industrial machinery and processes, reducing the need for human intervention. In the scope of industrialization, _____ is a step beyond mechanization. Whereas mechanization provided human operators with machinery to assist them with the physical requirements of work, _____ greatly reduces the need for human sensory and mental requirements as well.
 a. A4e
 b. AAAI
 c. A Stake in the Outcome
 d. Automation

6. _____ concern the operation of a facility, as opposed to maintenance, supply and distribution, health, and safety, emergency response, human resources, security, information technology and other infrastructural support organizations.

Personnel that make up 'operations' are

- operators
- engineers
- technicians
- management

This is mainly in a manufacturing setting.

 a. Conglomerate merger
 b. Labor intensive
 c. Manufacturing operations
 d. Market niche

Chapter 3. Enhancing Productivity: A Key to Sccess   21

7. The _____ is the labour pool in employment. It is generally used to describe those working for a single company or industry, but can also apply to a geographic region like a city, country, state, etc. The term generally excludes the employers or management, and implies those involved in manual labour.
   a. Work-life balance
   b. Pink-collar worker
   c. Division of labour
   d. Workforce

8. _____ is the amount of goods and services that a labourer produces in a given amount of time. It is one of several types of productivity that economists measure. _____ can be measured for a firm, a process or a country.
   a. Retroactive overtime
   b. Time and attendance
   c. Business Network Transformation
   d. Labour productivity

9. The _____ is a trilateral trade bloc in North America created by the governments of the United States, Canada, and Mexico. The agreement creating the trade bloc came into force on January 1, 1994. It superseded the Canada-United States Free Trade Agreement between the U.S. and Canada.
   a. Business war game
   b. Trade union
   c. Career portfolios
   d. North American Free Trade Agreement

10. _____ ('Plan-Do-Check-Act') is an iterative four-step problem-solving process typically used in business process improvement. It is also known as the Deming Cycle, Shewhart cycle, Deming Wheel, or Plan-Do-Study-Act.

    _____ was made popular by Dr. W. Edwards Deming, who is considered by many to be the father of modern quality control; however it was always referred to by him as the Shewhart cycle. Later in Deming's career, he modified _____ to Plan, Do, Study, Act (PDSA) so as to better describe his recommendations.

   a. Management by exception
   b. PDCA
   c. Management team
   d. Decentralization

11. In economics, business, retail, and accounting, a _____ is the value of money that has been used up to produce something, and hence is not available for use anymore. In economics, a _____ is an alternative that is given up as a result of a decision. In business, the _____ may be one of acquisition, in which case the amount of money expended to acquire it is counted as _____.

   a. Fixed costs
   b. Cost
   c. Cost overrun
   d. Cost allocation

12. An _____ is the negative aspects of human activity on the biophysical environment. Environmentalism, a social and environmental movement that started in the 1960s, focuses on addressing _____s through advocacy, education and activism.

Major current _____s are climate change, pollution and resource depletion.

   a. A4e
   b. AAAI
   c. A Stake in the Outcome
   d. Environmental issue

13. A _____ is a compensation, usually financial, received by a worker in exchange for their labor.

Compensation in terms of _____s is given to worker and compensation in terms of salary is given to employees. Compensation is a monetary benefits given to employees in returns of the services provided by them.

   a. Performance-related pay
   b. State Compensation Insurance Fund
   c. Wage
   d. Profit-sharing agreement

14. _____ is an advertisement in which a particular product specifically mentions a competitor by name for the express purpose of showing why the competitor is inferior to the product naming it.

This should not be confused with parody advertisements, where a fictional product is being advertised for the purpose of poking fun at the particular advertisement, nor should it be confused with the use of a coined brand name for the purpose of comparing the product without actually naming an actual competitor. ('Wikipedia tastes better and is less filling than the Encyclopedia Galactica.')

In the 1980s, during what has been referred to as the cola wars, soft-drink manufacturer Pepsi ran a series of advertisements where people, caught on hidden camera, in a blind taste test, chose Pepsi over rival Coca-Cola.

a. Comparative advertising
b. 28-hour day
c. 1990 Clean Air Act
d. 33 Strategies of War

15. A _____ is a plan for production, staffing, inventory, etc. It is usually linked to manufacturing where the plan indicates when and how much of each product will be demanded. This plan quantifies significant processes, parts, and other resources in order to optimize production, to identify bottlenecks, and to anticipate needs and completed goods.

a. Value engineering
b. Remanufacturing
c. Piecework
d. Master production schedule

16. A _____ or business method is a collection of related, structured activities or tasks that produce a specific service or product (serve a particular goal) for a particular customer or customers. It often can be visualized with a flowchart as a sequence of activities.

There are three types of _____es:

1. Management processes, the processes that govern the operation of a system. Typical management processes include 'Corporate Governance' and 'Strategic Management'.
2. Operational processes, processes that constitute the core business and create the primary value stream. Typical operational processes are Purchasing, Manufacturing, Marketing, and Sales.
3. Supporting processes, which support the core processes. Examples include Accounting, Recruitment, Technical support.

A _____ begins with a customer's need and ends with a customer's need fulfillment. Process oriented organizations break down the barriers of structural departments and try to avoid functional silos.

a. 33 Strategies of War
b. 28-hour day
c. 1990 Clean Air Act
d. Business process

Chapter 3. Enhancing Productivity: A Key to Sccess

17. _____, in microeconomics, are the cost advantages that a business obtains due to expansion. They are factors that cause a producer's average cost per unit to fall as scale is increased. _____ is a long run concept and refers to reductions in unit cost as the size of a facility, or scale, increases.

   a. Economies of scale
   b. Economies of scope
   c. A4e
   d. A Stake in the Outcome

18. _____ is an area of knowledge within organizational theory that studies models and theories about the way an organization learns and adapts.

In Organizational development (OD), learning is a characteristic of an adaptive organization, i.e., an organization that is able to sense changes in signals from its environment (both internal and external) and adapt accordingly.

   a. A4e
   b. Organizational learning
   c. A Stake in the Outcome
   d. AAAI

19. _____ is an increasingly broadening term with which an organization, or other human system describes the combination of traditionally administrative personnel functions with acquisition and application of skills, knowledge and experience, Employee Relations and resource planning at various levels. The field draws upon concepts developed in Industrial/Organizational Psychology and System Theory. _____ has at least two related interpretations depending on context. The original usage derives from political economy and economics, where it was traditionally called labor, one of four factors of production although this perspective is changing as a function of new and ongoing research into more strategic approaches at national levels. This first usage is used more in terms of '_____ development', and can go beyond just organizations to the level of nations . The more traditional usage within corporations and businesses refers to the individuals within a firm or agency, and to the portion of the organization that deals with hiring, firing, training, and other personnel issues, typically referred to as `_____ management'.
   a. Progressive discipline
   b. Human resources
   c. Human resource management
   d. Bradford Factor

20. In organizational development (OD), _____ is the application of Socio-Technical Systems principles and techniques to the humanization of work.

The aims of _____ to improved job satisfaction, to improved through-put, to improved quality and to reduced employee problems, e.g., grievances, absenteeism.

Under scientific management people would be directed by reason and the problems of industrial unrest would be appropriately (i.e., scientifically) addressed.

a. Management process
b. Path-goal theory
c. Work design
d. Graduate recruitment

Chapter 4. Quality Management

1. _____ is an advertisement in which a particular product specifically mentions a competitor by name for the express purpose of showing why the competitor is inferior to the product naming it.

This should not be confused with parody advertisements, where a fictional product is being advertised for the purpose of poking fun at the particular advertisement, nor should it be confused with the use of a coined brand name for the purpose of comparing the product without actually naming an actual competitor. ('Wikipedia tastes better and is less filling than the Encyclopedia Galactica.')

In the 1980s, during what has been referred to as the cola wars, soft-drink manufacturer Pepsi ran a series of advertisements where people, caught on hidden camera, in a blind taste test, chose Pepsi over rival Coca-Cola.

   a. 33 Strategies of War
   b. 1990 Clean Air Act
   c. 28-hour day
   d. Comparative advertising

2. The _____, widely known as ISO , is an international-standard-setting body composed of representatives from various national standards organizations. Founded on 23 February 1947, the organization promulgates worldwide proprietary industrial and commercial standards. It is headquartered in Geneva, Switzerland.
   a. AAAI
   b. A Stake in the Outcome
   c. A4e
   d. International Organization for Standardization

3. The _____ is a trilateral trade bloc in North America created by the governments of the United States, Canada, and Mexico. The agreement creating the trade bloc came into force on January 1, 1994. It superseded the Canada-United States Free Trade Agreement between the U.S. and Canada.
   a. Business war game
   b. Trade union
   c. North American Free Trade Agreement
   d. Career portfolios

4. Procter is a surname, and may also refer to:

   - Bryan Waller Procter (pseud. Barry Cornwall), English poet
   - Goodwin Procter, American law firm
   - _____, consumer products multinational

a. Strict liability
b. Master and Servant Acts
c. Downstream
d. Procter ' Gamble

5. In statistics, _____ refers to techniques for the modeling and analysis of numerical data consisting of values of a dependent variable and of one or more independent variables The dependent variable in the regression equation is modeled as a function of the independent variables, corresponding parameters, and an error term. The error term is treated as a random variable and represents unexplained variation in the dependent variable.
   a. Trend analysis
   b. Least squares
   c. Regression analysis
   d. Stepwise regression

6. In economics, business, retail, and accounting, a _____ is the value of money that has been used up to produce something, and hence is not available for use anymore. In economics, a _____ is an alternative that is given up as a result of a decision. In business, the _____ may be one of acquisition, in which case the amount of money expended to acquire it is counted as _____.
   a. Cost overrun
   b. Cost allocation
   c. Fixed costs
   d. Cost

7. The concept of quality costs is a means to quantify the total _____-related efforts and deficiencies. It was first described by Armand V. Feigenbaum in a 1956 Harvard Business Review article.

Prior to its introduction, the general perception was that higher quality requires higher costs, either by buying better materials or machines or by hiring more labor.

   a. Quality costs
   b. Cost of quality
   c. Fixed costs
   d. Cost accounting

8. _____ is a Japanese term that means 'fail-safing' or 'mistake-proofing'. A _____ is any mechanism in a Lean manufacturing process that helps an equipment operator avoid (yokeru) mistakes (poka.) Its purpose is to eliminate product defects by preventing, correcting, or drawing attention to human errors as they occur.

a. 28-hour day
b. 1990 Clean Air Act
c. 33 Strategies of War
d. Poka-yoke

9. _____ is a business management strategy, initially implemented by Motorola, that today enjoys widespread application in many sectors of industry.

_____ seeks to improve the quality of process outputs by identifying and removing the causes of defects (errors) and variation in manufacturing and business processes. It uses a set of quality management methods, including statistical methods, and creates a special infrastructure of people within the organization ('Black Belts' etc.)

a. Theory of constraints
b. Takt time
c. Six sigma
d. Production line

10. _____ can be considered to have three main components: quality control, quality assurance and quality improvement. _____ is focused not only on product quality, but also the means to achieve it. _____ therefore uses quality assurance and control of processes as well as products to achieve more consistent quality.

a. 1990 Clean Air Act
b. Quality management
c. 28-hour day
d. Total quality management

11. _____ are statistical methods developed by Genichi Taguchi to improve the quality of manufactured goods, and more recently also applied to biotechnology, marketing and advertising. Professional statisticians have welcomed the goals and improvements brought about by _____, particularly by Taguchi's development of designs for studying variation, but have criticized the inefficiency of some of Taguchi's proposals.

Taguchi's work includes three principal contributions to statistics:

1. Taguchi loss function;
2. The philosophy of off-line quality control; and
3. Innovations in the design of experiments.

Chapter 4. Quality Management

Traditionally, statistical methods have relied on mean-unbiased estimators of treatment effects: Under the conditions of the Gauss-Markov theorem, least squares estimators have minimum variance among all mean-unbiased estimators. The emphasis on comparisons of means also draws (limiting) comfort from the law of large numbers, according to which the sample means converge to the true mean.

a. Design of experiments
b. 1990 Clean Air Act
c. 28-hour day
d. Taguchi methods

12. _____ ('Plan-Do-Check-Act') is an iterative four-step problem-solving process typically used in business process improvement. It is also known as the Deming Cycle, Shewhart cycle, Deming Wheel, or Plan-Do-Study-Act.

_____ was made popular by Dr. W. Edwards Deming, who is considered by many to be the father of modern quality control; however it was always referred to by him as the Shewhart cycle. Later in Deming's career, he modified _____ to Plan, Do, Study, Act (PDSA) so as to better describe his recommendations.

a. Management team
b. Decentralization
c. Management by exception
d. PDCA

13. _____ is a business management strategy aimed at embedding awareness of quality in all organizational processes. _____ has been widely used in manufacturing, education, hospitals, call centers, government, and service industries, as well as NASA space and science programs.

As defined by the International Organization for Standardization (ISO):

'_____ is a management approach for an organization, centered on quality, based on the participation of all its members and aiming at long-term success through customer satisfaction, and benefits to all members of the organization and to society.' ISO 8402:1994

One major aim is to reduce variation from every process so that greater consistency of effort is obtained. (Royse, D., Thyer, B., Padgett D., ' Logan T., 2006)

a. 28-hour day
b. Quality management
c. 1990 Clean Air Act
d. Total quality management

14. _____ is a term used in business and Information Technology (through ITIL) to describe the process of capturing a customer's requirements. Specifically, the _____ is a market research technique that produces a detailed set of customer wants and needs, organized into a hierarchical structure, and then prioritized in terms of relative importance and satisfaction with current alternatives. _____ studies typically consist of both qualitative and quantitative research steps.

a. Business philosophy
b. Voice of the customer
c. Goal setting
d. Board of governors

15. _____ is a graphic tool for defining the relationship between customer desires and the firm/product capabilities. It is a part of the Quality Function Deployment (QFD) and it utilizes a planning matrix to relate what the customer wants to how a firm (that produce the products) is going to meet those wants. It looks like a House with correlation matrix as its roof, customer wants versus product features as the main part, competitor evaluation as the porch etc.

a. Decision Matrix
b. House of quality
c. Consensus-seeking decision-making
d. Health management system

16. _____ is a 'method to transform user demands into design quality, to deploy the functions forming quality, and to deploy methods for achieving the design quality into subsystems and component parts, and ultimately to specific elements of the manufacturing process.' , as described by Dr. Yoji Akao, who originally developed _____ in Japan in 1966, when the author combined his work in quality assurance and quality control points with function deployment used in Value Engineering.

_____ is designed to help planners focus on characteristics of a new or existing product or service from the viewpoints of market segments, company, or technology-development needs. The technique yields graphs and matrices.

a. Learning organization
b. Hoshin Kanri
c. 1990 Clean Air Act
d. Quality function deployment

Chapter 4. Quality Management

17. _____ is the process of comparing the cost, cycle time, productivity, or quality of a specific process or method to another that is widely considered to be an industry standard or best practice. Essentially, _____ provides a snapshot of the performance of your business and helps you understand where you are in relation to a particular standard. The result is often a business case for making changes in order to make improvements.
    a. Competitive heterogeneity
    b. Complementors
    c. Cost leadership
    d. Benchmarking

18. _____ is the process whereby an organization establishes the parameters within which programs, investments, and acquisitions are reaching the desired results. Performance Reference Model of the Federal Enterprise Architecture, 2005.

This process of measuring performance often requires the use of statistical evidence to determine progress toward specific defined organizational objectives.

There are many types of measurements.

    a. Workflow
    b. Crisis management
    c. Performance measurement
    d. CIFMS

19. _____ is a family of standards for quality management systems. _____ is maintained by ISO, the International Organization for Standardization and is administered by accreditation and certification bodies. The rules are updated, the time and changes in the requirements for quality, motivate change.
    a. AAAI
    b. A Stake in the Outcome
    c. A4e
    d. ISO 9000

20. In probability theory, a probability distribution is called _____ if its cumulative distribution function is _____. This is equivalent to saying that for random variables X with the distribution in question, Pr[X = a] = 0 for all real numbers a, i.e.: the probability that X attains the value a is zero, for any number a. If the distribution of X is _____ then X is called a _____ random variable.

a. Continuous
b. Decision tree pruning
c. Connectionist expert systems
d. Pay Band

21. _____ is a management process whereby delivery (customer valued) processes are constantly evaluated and improved in the light of their efficiency, effectiveness and flexibility.

Some see it as a meta process for most management systems (Business Process Management, Quality Management, Project Management). Deming saw it as part of the 'system' whereby feedback from the process and customer were evaluated against organisational goals.

   a. Continuous Improvement Process
   b. First-mover advantage
   c. Sole proprietorship
   d. Critical Success Factor

22. _____ is a Japanese philosophy that focuses on continuous improvement throughout all aspects of life. When applied to the workplace, _____ activities continually improve all functions of a business, from manufacturing to management and from the CEO to the assembly line workers. By improving standardized activities and processes, _____ aims to eliminate waste .
   a. Psychological pricing
   b. Sensitivity analysis
   c. Cross-docking
   d. Kaizen

23. The _____ is given by the United States National Institute of Standards and Technology. Through the actions of the National Productivity Advisory Committee chaired by Jack Grayson, it was established by the Malcolm Baldrige National Quality Improvement Act of 1987 - Public Law 100-107 and named for Malcolm Baldrige, who served as United States Secretary of Commerce during the Reagan administration from 1981 until his 1987 death in a rodeo accident. APQC, , organized the first White House Conference on Productivity, spearheading the creation and design of the _____ in 1987, and jointly administering the award for its first three years.
   a. Business Network Transformation
   b. Scenario planning
   c. Time and attendance
   d. Malcolm Baldrige National Quality Award

24. _____ is an organization's process of defining its strategy and making decisions on allocating its resources to pursue this strategy, including its capital and people. Various business analysis techniques can be used in _____, including SWOT analysis (Strengths, Weaknesses, Opportunities, and Threats) and PEST analysis (Political, Economic, Social, and Technological analysis) or STEER analysis involving Socio-cultural, Technological, Economic, Ecological, and Regulatory factors and EPISTEL (Environment, Political, Informatic, Social, Technological, Economic and Legal)

_____ is the formal consideration of an organization's future course. All _____ deals with at least one of three key questions:

1. 'What do we do?'
2. 'For whom do we do it?'
3. 'How do we excel?'

In business _____, the third question is better phrased 'How can we beat or avoid competition?'. (Bradford and Duncan, page 1.)

a. 1990 Clean Air Act
b. Strategic planning
c. 33 Strategies of War
d. 28-hour day

Chapter 5. Enterprise Integration and Supply Chain Management: A Strategic Perspective

1. A _____ is the system of organizations, people, technology, activities, information and resources involved in moving a product or service from supplier to customer. _____ activities transform natural resources, raw materials and components into a finished product that is delivered to the end customer. In sophisticated _____ systems, used products may re-enter the _____ at any point where residual value is recyclable.
   a. Packaging
   b. Drop shipping
   c. Wholesalers
   d. Supply chain

2. _____ is the management of a network of interconnected businesses involved in the ultimate provision of product and service packages required by end customers (Harland, 1996.) _____ spans all movement and storage of raw materials, work-in-process inventory, and finished goods from point of origin to point of consumption (supply chain.)

   The definition an American professional association put forward is that _____ encompasses the planning and management of all activities involved in sourcing, procurement, conversion, and logistics management activities.

   a. Drop shipping
   b. Packaging
   c. Freight forwarder
   d. Supply chain management

3. The _____, widely known as ISO, is an international-standard-setting body composed of representatives from various national standards organizations. Founded on 23 February 1947, the organization promulgates worldwide proprietary industrial and commercial standards. It is headquartered in Geneva, Switzerland.
   a. AAAI
   b. A4e
   c. A Stake in the Outcome
   d. International Organization for Standardization

4. _____ is the management of the flow of goods, information and other resources, including energy and people, between the point of origin and the point of consumption in order to meet the requirements of consumers (frequently, and originally, military organizations.) _____ involves the integration of information, transportation, inventory, warehousing, material-handling, and packaging, and occasionally security. _____ is a channel of the supply chain which adds the value of time and place utility.
   a. Third-party logistics
   b. Logistics
   c. 1990 Clean Air Act
   d. 28-hour day

Chapter 5. Enterprise Integration and Supply Chain Management: A Strategic Perspective

5. In statistics, _____ refers to techniques for the modeling and analysis of numerical data consisting of values of a dependent variable and of one or more independent variables The dependent variable in the regression equation is modeled as a function of the independent variables, corresponding parameters, and an error term. The error term is treated as a random variable and represents unexplained variation in the dependent variable.

   a. Trend analysis
   b. Least squares
   c. Stepwise regression
   d. Regression analysis

6. _____ stands for all operations related to the reuse of products and materials. It is 'the process of planning, implementing, and controlling the efficient, cost effective flow of raw materials, in-process inventory, finished goods and related information from the point of consumption to the point of origin for the purpose of recapturing value or proper disposal. More precisely, _____ is the process of moving goods from their typical final destination for the purpose of capturing value, or proper disposal.

   a. Reverse logistics
   b. 33 Strategies of War
   c. 28-hour day
   d. 1990 Clean Air Act

7. Procter is a surname, and may also refer to:

   - Bryan Waller Procter (pseud. Barry Cornwall), English poet
   - Goodwin Procter, American law firm
   - _____, consumer products multinational

   a. Master and Servant Acts
   b. Procter ' Gamble
   c. Downstream
   d. Strict liability

8. _____ are statistical methods developed by Genichi Taguchi to improve the quality of manufactured goods, and more recently also applied to biotechnology, marketing and advertising. Professional statisticians have welcomed the goals and improvements brought about by _____, particularly by Taguchi's development of designs for studying variation, but have criticized the inefficiency of some of Taguchi's proposals.

Chapter 5. Enterprise Integration and Supply Chain Management: A Strategic Perspective

Taguchi's work includes three principal contributions to statistics:

1. Taguchi loss function;
2. The philosophy of off-line quality control; and
3. Innovations in the design of experiments.

Traditionally, statistical methods have relied on mean-unbiased estimators of treatment effects: Under the conditions of the Gauss-Markov theorem, least squares estimators have minimum variance among all mean-unbiased estimators. The emphasis on comparisons of means also draws (limiting) comfort from the law of large numbers, according to which the sample means converge to the true mean.

a. Taguchi methods
b. 28-hour day
c. 1990 Clean Air Act
d. Design of experiments

9. The _____ is an observed phenomenon in forecast-driven distribution channels. The concept has its roots in J Forrester's Industrial Dynamics (1961) and thus it is also known as the Forrester Effect. Since the oscillating demand magnification upstream a supply chain reminds someone of a cracking whip it became famous as the _____.

a. 33 Strategies of War
b. 28-hour day
c. 1990 Clean Air Act
d. Bullwhip effect

10. _____ Management is the succession of strategies used by management as a product goes through its _____. The conditions in which a product is sold changes over time and must be managed as it moves through its succession of stages.

The _____ goes through many phases, involves many professional disciplines, and requires many skills, tools and processes.

a. Job hunting
b. Strategic Alliance
c. Golden handshake
d. Product life cycle

Chapter 5. Enterprise Integration and Supply Chain Management: A Strategic Perspective

11. In the fields of science, engineering, industry and statistics, _____ is the degree of closeness of a measured or calculated quantity to its actual (true) value. _____ is closely related to precision, also called reproducibility or repeatability, the degree to which further measurements or calculations show the same or similar results. _____ indicates proximity to the true value, precision to the repeatability or reproducibility of the measurement

The results of calculations or a measurement can be accurate but not precise, precise but not accurate, neither, or both.

   a. AAAI
   b. A4e
   c. A Stake in the Outcome
   d. Accuracy

12. _____ refers to the structured transmission of data between organizations by electronic means. It is used to transfer electronic documents from one computer system to another (ie) from one trading partner to another trading partner. It is more than mere E-mail; for instance, organizations might replace bills of lading and even checks with appropriate _____ messages.
   a. Electronic data interchange
   b. AAAI
   c. A4e
   d. A Stake in the Outcome

13. _____ is a concept that aims to enhance supply chain integration by supporting and assisting joint practices. _____ seeks cooperative management of inventory through joint visibility and replenishment of products throughout the supply chain. Information shared between suppliers and retailers aids in planning and satisfying customer demands through a supportive system of shared information.
   a. Timesheets
   b. Groups decision making
   c. Collaborative Planning, Forecasting and Replenishment
   d. Career portfolios

14. Manufacturing Resource Planning (_____) is defined by APICS as a method for the effective planning of all resources of a manufacturing company. Ideally, it addresses operational planning in units, financial planning in dollars, and has a simulation capability to answer 'what-if' questions and extension of closed-loop MRP. Manufacturing Resource Planning (or MRP2) - Around 1980, over-frequent changes in sales forecasts, entailing continual readjustments in production, as well as the unsuitability of the parameters fixed by the system, led MRP (Material Requirement Planning) to evolve into a new concept : Manufacturing Resource Planning (e.g. MRP 2)

This is not exclusively a software function, but a marriage of people skills, dedication to data base accuracy, and computer resources.

a. Jidoka
b. Manufacturing resource planning
c. Homeworkers
d. MRP II

15. _____ is an operational activity which does an aggregate plan for the production process, in advance of 2 to 18 months, to give an idea to management as to what quantity of materials and other resources are to be procured and when, so that the total cost of operations of the organization is kept to the minimum over that period.

The quantity of outsourcing, subcontracting of items, overtime of labor, numbers to be hired and fired in each period and the amount of inventory to be held in stock and to be backlogged for each period are decided. All of these activities are done within the framework of the company ethics, policies, and long term commitment to the society, community and the country of operation.

a. A Stake in the Outcome
b. Earned value management
c. Aggregate planning
d. Earned Schedule

16. _____ is one of the four elements of marketing mix. An organization or set of organizations (go-betweens) involved in the process of making a product or service available for use or consumption by a consumer or business user.

The other three parts of the marketing mix are product, pricing, and promotion.

a. Distribution
b. Job creation programs
c. Missing completely at random
d. Matching theory

17. _____ is a company-wide computer software system used to manage and coordinate all the resources, information, and functions of a business from shared data stores.

An _____ system has a service-oriented architecture with modular hardware and software units and 'services' that communicate on a local area network. The modular design allows a business to add or reconfigure modules (perhaps from different vendors) while preserving data integrity in one shared database that may be centralized or distributed.

Chapter 5. Enterprise Integration and Supply Chain Management: A Strategic Perspective

a. AAAI
b. A4e
c. Enterprise resource planning
d. A Stake in the Outcome

18. _____ is the process of estimation in unknown situations. Prediction is a similar, but more general term. Both can refer to estimation of time series, cross-sectional or longitudinal data.

a. 28-hour day
b. 33 Strategies of War
c. Forecasting
d. 1990 Clean Air Act

19. _____ is defined by APICS as a method for the effective planning of all resources of a manufacturing company. Ideally, it addresses operational planning in units, financial planning in dollars, and has a simulation capability to answer 'what-if' questions and extension of closed-loop _____. Manufacturing resource planning (or Manufacturing resource planning2) - Around 1980, over-frequent changes in sales forecasts, entailing continual readjustments in production, as well as the unsuitability of the parameters fixed by the system, led _____ (Material Requirement Planning) to evolve into a new concept : _____ (e.g. _____ 2)

This is not exclusively a software function, but a marriage of people skills, dedication to data base accuracy, and computer resources.

a. Jidoka
b. Homeworkers
c. MRP II
d. Manufacturing resource planning

20. _____ is a software based production planning and inventory control system used to manage manufacturing processes. Although it is not common nowadays, it is possible to conduct _____ by hand as well.

An _____ system is intended to simultaneously meet three objectives:

- Ensure materials and products are available for production and delivery to customers.
- Maintain the lowest possible level of inventory.
- Plan manufacturing activities, delivery schedules and purchasing activities.

Manufacturing organizations, whatever their products, face the same daily practical problem - that customers want products to be available in a shorter time than it takes to make them. This means that some level of planning is required.

Chapter 5. Enterprise Integration and Supply Chain Management: A Strategic Perspective

a. 33 Strategies of War
b. 1990 Clean Air Act
c. 28-hour day
d. Material requirements planning

21. _____ is an organization's process of defining its strategy and making decisions on allocating its resources to pursue this strategy, including its capital and people. Various business analysis techniques can be used in _____, including SWOT analysis (Strengths, Weaknesses, Opportunities, and Threats) and PEST analysis (Political, Economic, Social, and Technological analysis) or STEER analysis involving Socio-cultural, Technological, Economic, Ecological, and Regulatory factors and EPISTEL (Environment, Political, Informatic, Social, Technological, Economic and Legal)

_____ is the formal consideration of an organization's future course. All _____ deals with at least one of three key questions:

1. 'What do we do?'
2. 'For whom do we do it?'
3. 'How do we excel?'

In business _____, the third question is better phrased 'How can we beat or avoid competition?'. (Bradford and Duncan, page 1.)

a. 33 Strategies of War
b. 1990 Clean Air Act
c. 28-hour day
d. Strategic planning

22. Business-to-consumer describes activities of businesses serving end consumers with products and/or services.

An example of a _____ transaction would be a person buying a pair of shoes from a retailer. The transactions that led to the shoes being available for purchase, that is the purchase of the leather, laces, rubber, etc.

a. PEST analysis
b. Green marketing
c. Market environment
d. B2C

23. _____ in manufacturing refers to processes that occur later on in a production sequence or production line.

Viewing a company 'from order to cash' might have high-level processes such as Marketing, Sales, Order Entry, Manufacturing, Packaging, Shipping, Invoicing. Each of these could be deconstructed into many sub-processes and supporting processes.

a. Probability-generating function
b. Science Learning Centre
c. Genbutsu
d. Downstream

24. _____ is subcontracting a process, such as product design or manufacturing, to a third-party company. The decision to outsource is often made in the interest of lowering cost or making better use of time and energy costs, redirecting or conserving energy directed at the competencies of a particular business, or to make more efficient use of land, labor, capital, (information) technology and resources. _____ became part of the business lexicon during the 1980s.

a. Opinion leadership
b. Outsourcing
c. Operant conditioning
d. Unemployment insurance

25. In microeconomics and management, the term _____ describes a style of management control. Vertically integrated companies are united through a hierarchy with a common owner. Usually each member of the hierarchy produces a different product or (market-specific) service, and the products combine to satisfy a common need.

a. 1990 Clean Air Act
b. Vertical integration
c. 33 Strategies of War
d. 28-hour day

26. In economics, _____ is the removal of intermediaries in a supply chain: 'cutting out the middleman'. Instead of going through traditional distribution channels, which had some type of intermediate (such as a distributor, wholesaler, broker, or agent), companies may now deal with every customer directly, for example via the Internet. One important factor is a drop in the cost of servicing customers directly.

a. Virtual enterprise
b. 1990 Clean Air Act
c. 28-hour day
d. Disintermediation

Chapter 5. Enterprise Integration and Supply Chain Management: A Strategic Perspective

27. An _____ is the negative aspects of human activity on the biophysical environment. Environmentalism, a social and environmental movement that started in the 1960s, focuses on addressing _____s through advocacy, education and activism.

Major current _____s are climate change, pollution and resource depletion.

   a. A4e
   b. AAAI
   c. A Stake in the Outcome
   d. Environmental issue

28. In business and engineering, new _____ is the term used to describe the complete process of bringing a new product or service to market. There are two parallel paths involved in the NProduct development process: one involves the idea generation, product design, and detail engineering; the other involves market research and marketing analysis. Companies typically see new _____ as the first stage in generating and commercializing new products within the overall strategic process of product life cycle management used to maintain or grow their market share.
   a. 33 Strategies of War
   b. Product development
   c. 1990 Clean Air Act
   d. 28-hour day

29. A barcode (also bar code) is an optical machine-readable representation of data. Originally, _____ represented data in the widths (lines) and the spacings of parallel lines, and may be referred to as linear or 1D (1 dimensional) barcodes or symbologies. They also come in patterns of squares, dots, hexagons and other geometric patterns within images termed 2D (2 dimensional) matrix codes or symbologies.
   a. 28-hour day
   b. Bar codes
   c. 1990 Clean Air Act
   d. 33 Strategies of War

30. _____ of the learning curve effect and the closely related experience curve effect express the relationship between equations for experience and efficiency or between efficiency gains and investment in the effort. The experience of 'learning curves' was first observed by the 19th Century German psychologist Hermann Ebbinghaus according to the difficulty of memorizing varying numbers of verbal stimuli, and subsequent learning about the complex processes of learning are discussed in the

The rule used for representing the learning curve effect states that the more times a task has been performed, the less time will be required on each subsequent iteration.

a. Distribution
b. Point biserial correlation coefficient
c. Spatial Decision Support Systems
d. Models

31. _____ is a family of business models in which the buyer of a product provides certain information to a supplier of that product and the supplier takes full responsibility for maintaining an agreed inventory of the material, usually at the buyer's consumption location (usually a store.) A third party logistics provider can also be involved to make sure that the buyer has the required level of inventory by adjusting the demand and supply gaps.

As a symbiotic relationship, _____ makes it less likely that a business will unintentionally become out of stock of a good and reduces inventory in the supply chain.

a. Delayed differentiation
b. Supply-Chain Operations Reference
c. Supply Chain Risk Management
d. Vendor managed inventory

32. _____ or Postponement is a concept in supply chain management where the manufacturing process starts by making a generic or family product that is later differentiated into a specific end-product. This is a widely used method, especially in industries with high demand uncertainty, and can be effectively used to address the final demand even if forecasts cannot be improved.

An example would be Benetton and their knitted sweaters that are initially all white, and then dyed into different colors only when the season/customer color preference/demand is known.

a. Demand chain
b. Materials management
c. Supply-Chain Operations Reference
d. Delayed differentiation

33. _____, commonly known as e-commerce, consists of the buying and selling of products or services over electronic systems such as the Internet and other computer networks. The amount of trade conducted electronically has grown extraordinarily with widespread Internet usage. The use of commerce is conducted in this way, spurring and drawing on innovations in electronic funds transfer, supply chain management, Internet marketing, online transaction processing, electronic data interchange (EDI), inventory management systems, and automated data collection systems.

Chapter 5. Enterprise Integration and Supply Chain Management: A Strategic Perspective

   a. A4e
   b. Online shopping
   c. A Stake in the Outcome
   d. Electronic Commerce

34. A _____ is a type of business entity in which partners (owners) share with each other the profits or losses of the business. _____s are often favored over corporations for taxation purposes, as the _____ structure does not generally incur a tax on profits before it is distributed to the partners (i.e. there is no dividend tax levied.) However, depending on the _____ structure and the jurisdiction in which it operates, owners of a _____ may be exposed to greater personal liability than they would as shareholders of a corporation.
   a. Federal Employers Liability Act
   b. Due process
   c. Partnership
   d. Mediation

35. _____ refers to metrics and measures of output from production processes, per unit of input. Labor _____, for example, is typically measured as a ratio of output per labor-hour, an input. _____ may be conceived of as a metrics of the technical or engineering efficiency of production.
   a. Remanufacturing
   b. Value engineering
   c. Master production schedule
   d. Productivity

36. _____ describes commerce transactions between businesses, such as between a manufacturer and a wholesaler, or between a wholesaler and a retailer. Contrasting terms are business-to-consumer (B2C) and business-to-government (B2G.)

The volume of B2B transactions is much higher than the volume of B2C transactions.

   a. Product bundling
   b. Category management
   c. Market environment
   d. Business-to-business

37. _____ is the process whereby an organization establishes the parameters within which programs, investments, and acquisitions are reaching the desired results. Performance Reference Model of the Federal Enterprise Architecture, 2005.

Chapter 5. Enterprise Integration and Supply Chain Management: A Strategic Perspective

This process of measuring performance often requires the use of statistical evidence to determine progress toward specific defined organizational objectives.

There are many types of measurements.

a. Workflow
b. Performance measurement
c. Crisis management
d. CIFMS

Chapter 6. Product Development: A Team Approach

1. Procter is a surname, and may also refer to:

   - Bryan Waller Procter (pseud. Barry Cornwall), English poet
   - Goodwin Procter, American law firm
   - _____, consumer products multinational

   a. Procter ' Gamble
   b. Downstream
   c. Strict liability
   d. Master and Servant Acts

2. In business and engineering, new _____ is the term used to describe the complete process of bringing a new product or service to market. There are two parallel paths involved in the NProduct development process: one involves the idea generation, product design, and detail engineering; the other involves market research and marketing analysis. Companies typically see new _____ as the first stage in generating and commercializing new products within the overall strategic process of product life cycle management used to maintain or grow their market share.
   a. 28-hour day
   b. 1990 Clean Air Act
   c. 33 Strategies of War
   d. Product development

3. _____ ('Plan-Do-Check-Act') is an iterative four-step problem-solving process typically used in business process improvement. It is also known as the Deming Cycle, Shewhart cycle, Deming Wheel, or Plan-Do-Study-Act.

   _____ was made popular by Dr. W. Edwards Deming, who is considered by many to be the father of modern quality control; however it was always referred to by him as the Shewhart cycle. Later in Deming's career, he modified _____ to Plan, Do, Study, Act (PDSA) so as to better describe his recommendations.

   a. Management by exception
   b. Management team
   c. Decentralization
   d. PDCA

4. _____ Management is the succession of strategies used by management as a product goes through its _____. The conditions in which a product is sold changes over time and must be managed as it moves through its succession of stages.

   The _____ goes through many phases, involves many professional disciplines, and requires many skills, tools and processes.

Chapter 6. Product Development: A Team Approach

   a. Golden handshake
   b. Job hunting
   c. Strategic Alliance
   d. Product life cycle

5. _____ are statistical methods developed by Genichi Taguchi to improve the quality of manufactured goods, and more recently also applied to biotechnology, marketing and advertising. Professional statisticians have welcomed the goals and improvements brought about by _____, particularly by Taguchi's development of designs for studying variation, but have criticized the inefficiency of some of Taguchi's proposals.

Taguchi's work includes three principal contributions to statistics:

1. Taguchi loss function;
2. The philosophy of off-line quality control; and
3. Innovations in the design of experiments.

Traditionally, statistical methods have relied on mean-unbiased estimators of treatment effects: Under the conditions of the Gauss-Markov theorem, least squares estimators have minimum variance among all mean-unbiased estimators. The emphasis on comparisons of means also draws (limiting) comfort from the law of large numbers, according to which the sample means converge to the true mean.

   a. Taguchi methods
   b. Design of experiments
   c. 28-hour day
   d. 1990 Clean Air Act

6. In economics, business, retail, and accounting, a _____ is the value of money that has been used up to produce something, and hence is not available for use anymore. In economics, a _____ is an alternative that is given up as a result of a decision. In business, the _____ may be one of acquisition, in which case the amount of money expended to acquire it is counted as _____.
   a. Cost overrun
   b. Cost allocation
   c. Fixed costs
   d. Cost

7. _____ is the provision of service to customers before, during and after a purchase.

According to Turban et al. (2002), '_____ is a series of activities designed to enhance the level of customer satisfaction - that is, the feeling that a product or service has met the customer expectation.'

Its importance varies by product, industry and customer; defective or broken merchandise can be exchanged, often only with a receipt and within a specified time frame.

a. 28-hour day
b. 1990 Clean Air Act
c. Service rate
d. Customer service

8. A _____ is a documented investigation of a Market that is used to inform a firm's planning activities particularly around decision of: inventory, purchase, work force expansion/contraction, facility expansion, purchases of capital equipment, promotional activities, and many other aspects of a company.

Not all managers are asked to conduct a _____, but all managers must make decisions using _____ data and understand how the data was derived. So all managers need a reasonable understanding of the tools most used for making sales forecasts and analyzing markets.

a. Marketing research process
b. Marketing research
c. Market analysis
d. 1990 Clean Air Act

9. _____ is an advertisement in which a particular product specifically mentions a competitor by name for the express purpose of showing why the competitor is inferior to the product naming it.

This should not be confused with parody advertisements, where a fictional product is being advertised for the purpose of poking fun at the particular advertisement, nor should it be confused with the use of a coined brand name for the purpose of comparing the product without actually naming an actual competitor. ('Wikipedia tastes better and is less filling than the Encyclopedia Galactica.')

In the 1980s, during what has been referred to as the cola wars, soft-drink manufacturer Pepsi ran a series of advertisements where people, caught on hidden camera, in a blind taste test, chose Pepsi over rival Coca-Cola.

a. 33 Strategies of War
b. 28-hour day
c. 1990 Clean Air Act
d. Comparative advertising

Chapter 6. Product Development: A Team Approach 49

10. _____ is a strategic planning method used to evaluate the Strengths, Weaknesses, Opportunities, and Threats involved in a project or in a business venture. It involves specifying the objective of the business venture or project and identifying the internal and external factors that are favorable and unfavorable to achieving that objective. The technique is credited to Albert Humphrey, who led a convention at Stanford University in the 1960s and 1970s using data from Fortune 500 companies.
   a. SWOT analysis
   b. Market share
   c. Marketing
   d. Corporate image

11. _____ is used for the design, development, analysis, and optimization of technical processes and is mainly applied to chemical plants and chemical processes, but also to power stations, and similar technical facilities. Process flow diagram of a typical amine treating process used in industrial plants

   _____ is a model-based representation of chemical, physical, biological, and other technical processes and unit operations in software. Basic prerequisites are a thorough knowledge of chemical and physical properties of pure components and mixtures, of reactions, and of mathematical models which, in combination, allow the calculation of a process in computers.

   a. 33 Strategies of War
   b. Process simulation
   c. 28-hour day
   d. 1990 Clean Air Act

12. _____ is a method of planning and managing projects that puts the main emphasis on the resources required to execute project tasks. It was developed by Eliyahu M. Goldratt. This is in contrast to the more traditional Critical Path and PERT methods, which emphasize task order and rigid scheduling. A Critical Chain project network will tend to keep the resources levelly loaded, but will require them to be flexible in their start times and to quickly switch between tasks and task chains to keep the whole project on schedule.
   a. Project engineer
   b. Critical Chain Project Management
   c. Project management office
   d. Precedence diagram

13. _____ is subcontracting a process, such as product design or manufacturing, to a third-party company. The decision to outsource is often made in the interest of lowering cost or making better use of time and energy costs, redirecting or conserving energy directed at the competencies of a particular business, or to make more efficient use of land, labor, capital, (information) technology and resources. _____ became part of the business lexicon during the 1980s.

Chapter 6. Product Development: A Team Approach

a. Operant conditioning
b. Unemployment insurance
c. Opinion leadership
d. Outsourcing

14. In systems engineering, _____ is an approach that subdivides a system into smaller parts (modules) that can be independently created and then used in different systems to drive multiple functionalities. Besides reduction in cost (due to lesser customization, and less learning time), and flexibility in design, modularity offers other benefits such as augmentation (adding new solution by merely plugging in a new module), and exclusion. Examples of modular systems are cars, computers and high rise buildings.
    a. 1990 Clean Air Act
    b. Statement of work
    c. Modular design
    d. 28-hour day

15. The _____, widely known as ISO , is an international-standard-setting body composed of representatives from various national standards organizations. Founded on 23 February 1947, the organization promulgates worldwide proprietary industrial and commercial standards. It is headquartered in Geneva, Switzerland.
    a. A4e
    b. AAAI
    c. A Stake in the Outcome
    d. International Organization for Standardization

16. _____, in microeconomics, are the cost advantages that a business obtains due to expansion. They are factors that cause a producer's average cost per unit to fall as scale is increased. _____ is a long run concept and refers to reductions in unit cost as the size of a facility, or scale, increases.
    a. Economies of scope
    b. A4e
    c. A Stake in the Outcome
    d. Economies of scale

17. In statistics, _____ refers to techniques for the modeling and analysis of numerical data consisting of values of a dependent variable and of one or more independent variables The dependent variable in the regression equation is modeled as a function of the independent variables, corresponding parameters, and an error term. The error term is treated as a random variable and represents unexplained variation in the dependent variable.

a. Trend analysis
b. Regression analysis
c. Stepwise regression
d. Least squares

18. _____ is a graphic tool for defining the relationship between customer desires and the firm/product capabilities. It is a part of the Quality Function Deployment (QFD) and it utilizes a planning matrix to relate what the customer wants to how a firm (that produce the products) is going to meet those wants. It looks like a House with correlation matrix as its roof, customer wants versus product features as the main part, competitor evaluation as the porch etc.

a. Decision Matrix
b. Consensus-seeking decision-making
c. Health management system
d. House of quality

19. _____ is a 'method to transform user demands into design quality, to deploy the functions forming quality, and to deploy methods for achieving the design quality into subsystems and component parts, and ultimately to specific elements of the manufacturing process.' , as described by Dr. Yoji Akao, who originally developed _____ in Japan in 1966, when the author combined his work in quality assurance and quality control points with function deployment used in Value Engineering.

_____ is designed to help planners focus on characteristics of a new or existing product or service from the viewpoints of market segments, company, or technology-development needs. The technique yields graphs and matrices.

a. Learning organization
b. Hoshin Kanri
c. 1990 Clean Air Act
d. Quality function deployment

Chapter 7. Models and Forecasting

1. _____ is the process of estimation in unknown situations. Prediction is a similar, but more general term. Both can refer to estimation of time series, cross-sectional or longitudinal data.
   a. 33 Strategies of War
   b. 1990 Clean Air Act
   c. Forecasting
   d. 28-hour day

2. _____ of the learning curve effect and the closely related experience curve effect express the relationship between equations for experience and efficiency or between efficiency gains and investment in the effort. The experience of 'learning curves' was first observed by the 19th Century German psychologist Hermann Ebbinghaus according to the difficulty of memorizing varying numbers of verbal stimuli, and subsequent learning about the complex processes of learning are discussed in the

   .

   The rule used for representing the learning curve effect states that the more times a task has been performed, the less time will be required on each subsequent iteration.

   a. Models
   b. Point biserial correlation coefficient
   c. Distribution
   d. Spatial Decision Support Systems

3. _____ is a concept that aims to enhance supply chain integration by supporting and assisting joint practices. _____ seeks cooperative management of inventory through joint visibility and replenishment of products throughout the supply chain. Information shared between suppliers and retailers aids in planning and satisfying customer demands through a supportive system of shared information.
   a. Career portfolios
   b. Timesheets
   c. Groups decision making
   d. Collaborative Planning, Forecasting and Replenishment

4. The _____ is a systematic, interactive forecasting method which relies on a panel of independent experts. The carefully selected experts answer questionnaires in two or more rounds. After each round, a facilitator provides an anonymous summary of the experts' forecasts from the previous round as well as the reasons they provided for their judgments.

Chapter 7. Models and Forecasting

a. Quality function deployment
b. Delphi method
c. Learning organization
d. Hoshin Kanri

5. _____ are statistical methods developed by Genichi Taguchi to improve the quality of manufactured goods, and more recently also applied to biotechnology, marketing and advertising. Professional statisticians have welcomed the goals and improvements brought about by _____, particularly by Taguchi's development of designs for studying variation, but have criticized the inefficiency of some of Taguchi's proposals.

Taguchi's work includes three principal contributions to statistics:

1. Taguchi loss function;
2. The philosophy of off-line quality control; and
3. Innovations in the design of experiments.

Traditionally, statistical methods have relied on mean-unbiased estimators of treatment effects: Under the conditions of the Gauss-Markov theorem, least squares estimators have minimum variance among all mean-unbiased estimators. The emphasis on comparisons of means also draws (limiting) comfort from the law of large numbers, according to which the sample means converge to the true mean.

a. Design of experiments
b. 28-hour day
c. Taguchi methods
d. 1990 Clean Air Act

6. _____ is an integrated communications-based process through which individuals and communities discover that existing and newly-identified needs and wants may be satisfied by the products and services of others.

_____ is defined by the American _____ Association as the activity, set of institutions, and processes for creating, communicating, delivering, and exchanging offerings that have value for customers, clients, partners, and society at large. The term developed from the original meaning which referred literally to going to market, as in shopping, or going to a market to buy or sell goods or services.

a. Marketing
b. Disruptive technology
c. Market development
d. Customer relationship management

Chapter 7. Models and Forecasting

7. A _____, in the field of business and marketing, is a geographic region or demographic group used to gauge the viability of a product or service in the mass market prior to a wide scale roll-out. The criteria used to judge the acceptability of a _____ region or group include:

1. a population that is demographically similar to the proposed target market; and
2. relative isolation from densely populated media markets so that advertising to the test audience can be efficient and economical.

The _____ ideally aims to duplicate 'everything' - promotion and distribution as well as `product` - on a smaller scale. The technique replicates, typically in one area, what is planned to occur in a national launch; and the results are very carefully monitored, so that they can be extrapolated to projected national results. The `area` may be any one of the following:

- Television area

internet online test

- Test town
- Residential neighborhood
- Test site

A number of decisions have to be taken about any _____:

- Which _____?
- What is to be tested?
- How long a test?
- What are the success criteria?

The simple go or no-go decision, together with the related reduction of risk, is normally the main justification for the expense of _____s. At the same time, however, such _____s can be used to test specific elements of a new product's marketing mix; possibly the version of the product itself, the promotional message and media spend, the distribution channels and the price.

a. Test market
b. 1990 Clean Air Act
c. 33 Strategies of War
d. 28-hour day

8. In statistics, a _____ rolling mean or running average, is a type of finite impulse response filter used to analyze a set of data points by creating a series of averages of different subsets of the full data set. A _____ is not a single number, but it is a set of numbers, each of which is the average of the corresponding subset of a larger set of data points. A _____ may also use unequal weights for each data value in the subset to emphasize particular values in the subset.

a. Standard deviation
b. Homoscedastic
c. Time series analysis
d. Moving average

9. A _____ is the unweighted mean of the previous n data points. For example, a 10-day _____ of closing price is the mean of the previous 10 days' closing prices. If those prices are $p_M, p_{M-1}, \ldots, p_{M-9}$ then the formula is

$$SMA = \frac{p_M + p_{M-1} + \cdots + p_{M-9}}{10}$$

When calculating successive values, a new value comes into the sum and an old value drops out, meaning a full summation each time is unnecessary,

$$SMA_{\text{today}} = SMA_{\text{yesterday}} - \frac{p_{M-n}}{n} + \frac{p_M}{n}$$

In technical analysis there are various popular values for n, like 10 days, 40 days, or 200 days.

a. Descriptive statistics
b. Statistically significant
c. Confidence interval
d. Simple moving average

10. In statistics, _____ is a technique that can be applied to time series data, either to produce smoothed data for presentation, or to make forecasts. The time series data themselves are a sequence of observations. The observed phenomenon may be an essentially random process, or it may be an orderly, but noisy, process.
a. A Stake in the Outcome
b. AAAI
c. A4e
d. Exponential smoothing

11. In statistics and image processing, to smooth a data set is to create an approximating function that attempts to capture important patterns in the data, while leaving out noise or other fine-scale structures/rapid phenomena. Many different algorithms are used in _____. One of the most common algorithms is the 'moving average', often used to try to capture important trends in repeated statistical surveys.

a. 33 Strategies of War
b. 1990 Clean Air Act
c. Smoothing
d. 28-hour day

12. _____ ('Plan-Do-Check-Act') is an iterative four-step problem-solving process typically used in business process improvement. It is also known as the Deming Cycle, Shewhart cycle, Deming Wheel, or Plan-Do-Study-Act.

_____ was made popular by Dr. W. Edwards Deming, who is considered by many to be the father of modern quality control; however it was always referred to by him as the Shewhart cycle. Later in Deming's career, he modified _____ to Plan, Do, Study, Act (PDSA) so as to better describe his recommendations.

a. Management by exception
b. PDCA
c. Decentralization
d. Management team

13. The _____, widely known as ISO , is an international-standard-setting body composed of representatives from various national standards organizations. Founded on 23 February 1947, the organization promulgates worldwide proprietary industrial and commercial standards. It is headquartered in Geneva, Switzerland.
a. A Stake in the Outcome
b. A4e
c. AAAI
d. International Organization for Standardization

14. In statistics, _____ indicates the strength and direction of a linear relationship between two random variables. That is in contrast with the usage of the term in colloquial speech, which denotes any relationship, not necessarily linear. In general statistical usage, _____ or co-relation refers to the departure of two random variables from independence.
a. Heteroskedastic
b. Median
c. Time series analysis
d. Correlation

15. The terms '_____' and 'independent variable' are used in similar but subtly different ways in mathematics and statistics as part of the standard terminology in those subjects. They are used to distinguish between two types of quantities being considered, separating them into those available at the start of a process and those being created by it, where the latter (_____s) are dependent on the former (independent variables.)

Chapter 7. Models and Forecasting

The independent variable is typically the variable being manipulated or changed and the _____ is the observed result of the independent variable being manipulated.

a. Taguchi methods
b. 28-hour day
c. Dependent variable
d. 1990 Clean Air Act

16. In statistics, _____ refers to techniques for the modeling and analysis of numerical data consisting of values of a dependent variable and of one or more independent variables The dependent variable in the regression equation is modeled as a function of the independent variables, corresponding parameters, and an error term. The error term is treated as a random variable and represents unexplained variation in the dependent variable.
    a. Stepwise regression
    b. Least squares
    c. Trend analysis
    d. Regression analysis

17. _____ is a strategic planning method used to evaluate the Strengths, Weaknesses, Opportunities, and Threats involved in a project or in a business venture. It involves specifying the objective of the business venture or project and identifying the internal and external factors that are favorable and unfavorable to achieving that objective. The technique is credited to Albert Humphrey, who led a convention at Stanford University in the 1960s and 1970s using data from Fortune 500 companies.
    a. SWOT analysis
    b. Market share
    c. Corporate image
    d. Marketing

18. In the fields of science, engineering, industry and statistics, _____ is the degree of closeness of a measured or calculated quantity to its actual (true) value. _____ is closely related to precision, also called reproducibility or repeatability, the degree to which further measurements or calculations show the same or similar results. _____ indicates proximity to the true value, precision to the repeatability or reproducibility of the measurement

The results of calculations or a measurement can be accurate but not precise, precise but not accurate, neither, or both.

a. A4e
b. A Stake in the Outcome
c. AAAI
d. Accuracy

19. In statistics, _____ is:

- the arithmetic _____
- the expected value of a random variable, which is also called the population _____.

It is sometimes stated that the '_____' _____s average. This is incorrect if '_____' is taken in the specific sense of 'arithmetic _____' as there are different types of averages: the _____, median, and mode. Other simple statistical analyses use measures of spread, such as range, interquartile range, or standard deviation. For a real-valued random variable X, the _____ is the expectation of X. Note that not every probability distribution has a defined _____; see the Cauchy distribution for an example.

a. Statistical inference
b. Control chart
c. Correlation
d. Mean

20. In statistics, the _____ of an estimator is one of many ways to quantify the amount by which an estimator differs from the true value of the quantity being estimated. As a loss function, _____ is called squared error loss. _____ measures the average of the square of the 'error.' The error is the amount by which the estimator differs from the quantity to be estimated.

a. Mean squared error
b. 1990 Clean Air Act
c. 33 Strategies of War
d. 28-hour day

21. The _____ or simply average deviation of a data set is the average of the absolute deviations and is a summary statistic of statistical dispersion or variability. It is also called the mean absolute deviation, but this is easily confused with the median absolute deviation.

The average absolute deviation of a set $\{x_1, x_2, ..., x_n\}$ is

$\boxed{\times}$ >

The choice of measure of central tendency, m(X), has a marked effect on the value of the average deviation.

   a. AAAI
   b. A Stake in the Outcome
   c. A4e
   d. Average absolute deviation,

Chapter 8. Process Selection: Volume Drives Costs and Profits

1. The _____ is a trilateral trade bloc in North America created by the governments of the United States, Canada, and Mexico. The agreement creating the trade bloc came into force on January 1, 1994. It superseded the Canada-United States Free Trade Agreement between the U.S. and Canada.
   a. North American Free Trade Agreement
   b. Business war game
   c. Career portfolios
   d. Trade union

2. Procter is a surname, and may also refer to:

   - Bryan Waller Procter (pseud. Barry Cornwall), English poet
   - Goodwin Procter, American law firm
   - _____, consumer products multinational

   a. Master and Servant Acts
   b. Strict liability
   c. Downstream
   d. Procter ' Gamble

3. _____ can be defined as the idea generation, concept development, testing and manufacturing or implementation of a physical object or service. _____ers conceptualize and evaluate ideas, making them tangible through products in a more systematic approach. The role of a _____er encompasses many characteristics of the marketing manager, product manager, industrial designer and design engineer.
   a. Product design
   b. Adam Smith
   c. Affiliation
   d. Abraham Harold Maslow

4. _____ are statistical methods developed by Genichi Taguchi to improve the quality of manufactured goods, and more recently also applied to biotechnology, marketing and advertising. Professional statisticians have welcomed the goals and improvements brought about by _____, particularly by Taguchi's development of designs for studying variation, but have criticized the inefficiency of some of Taguchi's proposals.

Taguchi's work includes three principal contributions to statistics:

   1. Taguchi loss function;
   2. The philosophy of off-line quality control; and
   3. Innovations in the design of experiments.

Chapter 8. Process Selection: Volume Drives Costs and Profits

Traditionally, statistical methods have relied on mean-unbiased estimators of treatment effects: Under the conditions of the Gauss-Markov theorem, least squares estimators have minimum variance among all mean-unbiased estimators. The emphasis on comparisons of means also draws (limiting) comfort from the law of large numbers, according to which the sample means converge to the true mean.

a. Design of experiments
b. 1990 Clean Air Act
c. Taguchi methods
d. 28-hour day

5. In economics, business, retail, and accounting, a _____ is the value of money that has been used up to produce something, and hence is not available for use anymore. In economics, a _____ is an alternative that is given up as a result of a decision. In business, the _____ may be one of acquisition, in which case the amount of money expended to acquire it is counted as _____.
a. Cost overrun
b. Cost allocation
c. Fixed costs
d. Cost

6. The _____ of a product is the cost per standard unit supplied, which may be a single sample or a container of a given number. When purchasing more than a single unit, the total cost will increase with the number of units, but it is common for the _____ to decrease as quantity is increased (bulk purchasing), as there are discounts etc. This reduction in long run _____s which arise from an increase in production/purchasing is due to the fixed costs being spread out over more products and is called economies of scale.
a. Unit cost
b. AAAI
c. A4e
d. A Stake in the Outcome

7. _____ is a concept that aims to enhance supply chain integration by supporting and assisting joint practices. _____ seeks cooperative management of inventory through joint visibility and replenishment of products throughout the supply chain. Information shared between suppliers and retailers aids in planning and satisfying customer demands through a supportive system of shared information.
a. Groups decision making
b. Career portfolios
c. Timesheets
d. Collaborative Planning, Forecasting and Replenishment

62 *Chapter 8. Process Selection: Volume Drives Costs and Profits*

8. In economics, and cost accounting, _____ describes the total economic cost of production and is made up of variable costs, which vary according to the quantity of a good produced and include inputs such as labor and raw materials, plus fixed costs, which are independent of the quantity of a good produced and include inputs (capital) that cannot be varied in the short term, such as buildings and machinery. _____ in economics includes the total opportunity cost of each factor of production in addition to fixed and variable costs.

The rate at which _____ changes as the amount produced changes is called marginal cost.

   a. 33 Strategies of War
   b. Total cost
   c. 1990 Clean Air Act
   d. 28-hour day

9. _____, in microeconomics, are the cost advantages that a business obtains due to expansion. They are factors that cause a producer's average cost per unit to fall as scale is increased. _____ is a long run concept and refers to reductions in unit cost as the size of a facility, or scale, increases.
   a. Economies of scope
   b. Economies of scale
   c. A4e
   d. A Stake in the Outcome

10. _____ is the production of large amounts of standardized products, including and especially on assembly lines. The concepts of _____ are applied to various kinds of products, from fluids and particulates handled in bulk to discrete solid parts to assemblies of such parts

_____ of assemblies typically uses electric-motor-powered moving tracks or conveyor belts to move partially complete products to workers, who perform simple repetitive tasks.

   a. 1990 Clean Air Act
   b. 33 Strategies of War
   c. 28-hour day
   d. Mass production

11. The _____, widely known as ISO , is an international-standard-setting body composed of representatives from various national standards organizations. Founded on 23 February 1947, the organization promulgates worldwide proprietary industrial and commercial standards. It is headquartered in Geneva, Switzerland.

a. International Organization for Standardization
b. A Stake in the Outcome
c. A4e
d. AAAI

12. In probability theory, a probability distribution is called _____ if its cumulative distribution function is _____. This is equivalent to saying that for random variables X with the distribution in question, Pr[X = a] = 0 for all real numbers a, i.e.: the probability that X attains the value a is zero, for any number a. If the distribution of X is _____ then X is called a _____ random variable.
    a. Connectionist expert systems
    b. Pay Band
    c. Decision tree pruning
    d. Continuous

13. _____ is an overall management philosophy introduced by Dr. Eliyahu M. Goldratt in his 1984 book titled The Goal, that is geared to help organizations continually achieve their goal. The title comes from the contention that any manageable system is limited in achieving more of its goal by a very small number of constraints, and that there is always at least one constraint. The _____ process seeks to identify the constraint and restructure the rest of the organization around it, through the use of the Five Focusing Steps.
    a. Takt time
    b. Six Sigma
    c. Production line
    d. Theory of constraints

14. _____ are typically small manufacturing operations that handle specialized manufacturing processes such as small customer orders or small batch jobs. _____ typically move on to different jobs (possibly with different customers) when each job is completed. By nature of this type of manufacturing operation, _____ are usually specialized in skill and processes.
    a. 1990 Clean Air Act
    b. 33 Strategies of War
    c. 28-hour day
    d. Job shops

15. _____ refers to the movement of cash into or out of a business or financial product. It is usually measured during a specified, finite period of time. Measurement of _____ can be used

- to determine a project's rate of return or value. The time of _____s into and out of projects are used as inputs in financial models such as internal rate of return, and net present value.
- to determine problems with a business's liquidity. Being profitable does not necessarily mean being liquid. A company can fail because of a shortage of cash, even while profitable.
- as an alternate measure of a business's profits when it is believed that accrual accounting concepts do not represent economic realities. For example, a company may be notionally profitable but generating little operational cash (as may be the case for a company that barters its products rather than selling for cash.) In such a case, the company may be deriving additional operating cash by issuing shares evaluating default risk, re-investment requirements, etc.

_____ is a generic term used differently depending on the context. It may be defined by users for their own purposes.

a. Gross profit margin
b. Cash flow
c. Sweat equity
d. Gross profit

16. _____ is the discipline of planning, organizing and managing resources to bring about the successful completion of specific project goals and objectives. It is often closely related to and sometimes conflated with Program management.

A project is a finite endeavor--having specific start and completion dates--undertaken to meet particular goals and objectives, usually to bring about beneficial change or added value.

a. Project engineer
b. Precedence diagram
c. Project management
d. Work package

17. _____ is a model for workplace design, and is an integral part of lean manufacturing systems. The goal of lean manufacturing is the aggressive minimisation of waste, called muda, to achieve maximum efficiency of resources. _____, sometimes called cellular or cell production, arranges factory floor labor into semi-autonomous and multi-skilled teams, or work cells, who manufacture complete products or complex components.

a. Remanufacturing
b. Scientific management
c. Productivity
d. Cellular manufacturing

Chapter 8. Process Selection: Volume Drives Costs and Profits

18. _____, in marketing, manufacturing, call centres and management, is the use of flexible computer-aided manufacturing systems to produce custom output. Those systems combine the low unit costs of mass production processes with the flexibility of individual customization.

'_____' is the new frontier in business competition for both manufacturing and service industries.

  a. 1990 Clean Air Act
  b. Mass customization
  c. 33 Strategies of War
  d. 28-hour day

19. The _____ of 1938 (_____, ch. 676, 52 Stat. 1060, June 25, 1938, 29 U.S.C. ch.8), also called the Wages and Hours Bill, is United States federal law that applies to employees engaged in interstate commerce or employed by an enterprise engaged in commerce or in the production of goods for commerce, unless the employer can claim an exemption from coverage. The _____ established a national minimum wage, guaranteed time and a half for overtime in certain jobs, and prohibited most employment of minors in 'oppressive child labor,' a term defined in the statute.
  a. Joint venture
  b. Fair Labor Standards Act
  c. Family and Medical Leave Act of 1993
  d. Board of directors

20. _____ are conventions, treaties and recommendations designed to eliminate unjust and inhumane labour practices. The primary inernational agency charged with developing such standards is the International Labour Organization (ILO.) Established in 1919, the ILO advocates international standards as essential for the eradication of labour conditions involving 'injustice, hardship and privation'.
  a. Airbus SAS
  b. Anaconda Copper
  c. International labour standards
  d. Airbus Industrie

21. A _____ system is a manufacturing system in which there is some amount of flexibility that allows the system to react in the case of changes, whether predicted or unpredicted. This flexibility is generally considered to fall into two categories, which both contain numerous subcategories.

The first category, machine flexibility, covers the system's ability to be changed to produce new product types, and ability to change the order of operations executed on a part. The second category is called routing flexibility, which consists of the ability to use multiple machines to perform the same operation on a part, as well as the system's ability to absorb large-scale changes, such as in volume, capacity, or capability.

a. Manufacturing resource planning
b. Jidoka
c. Homeworkers
d. Flexible manufacturing

22. _____ is the use of control systems (such as numerical control, programmable logic control, and other industrial control systems), in concert with other applications of information technology (such as computer-aided technologies [CAD, CAM, CAx]), to control industrial machinery and processes, reducing the need for human intervention. In the scope of industrialization, _____ is a step beyond mechanization. Whereas mechanization provided human operators with machinery to assist them with the physical requirements of work, _____ greatly reduces the need for human sensory and mental requirements as well.
    a. Automation
    b. A Stake in the Outcome
    c. AAAI
    d. A4e

23. _____ is the body of laws, administrative rulings, and precedents which address the legal rights of, and restrictions on, working people and their organizations. As such, it mediates many aspects of the relationship between trade unions, employers and employees. In Canada, employment laws related to unionized workplaces are differentiated from those relating to particular individuals.
    a. Trade union
    b. Labor law
    c. Shift work
    d. Four-day week

24. _____ is an area of knowledge within organizational theory that studies models and theories about the way an organization learns and adapts.

In Organizational development (OD), learning is a characteristic of an adaptive organization, i.e., an organization that is able to sense changes in signals from its environment (both internal and external) and adapt accordingly.

    a. A4e
    b. AAAI
    c. A Stake in the Outcome
    d. Organizational learning

Chapter 9. Capacity Decisions

1. _____ are statistical methods developed by Genichi Taguchi to improve the quality of manufactured goods, and more recently also applied to biotechnology, marketing and advertising. Professional statisticians have welcomed the goals and improvements brought about by _____, particularly by Taguchi's development of designs for studying variation, but have criticized the inefficiency of some of Taguchi's proposals.

Taguchi's work includes three principal contributions to statistics:

1. Taguchi loss function;
2. The philosophy of off-line quality control; and
3. Innovations in the design of experiments.

Traditionally, statistical methods have relied on mean-unbiased estimators of treatment effects: Under the conditions of the Gauss-Markov theorem, least squares estimators have minimum variance among all mean-unbiased estimators. The emphasis on comparisons of means also draws (limiting) comfort from the law of large numbers, according to which the sample means converge to the true mean.

  a. Taguchi methods
  b. Design of experiments
  c. 1990 Clean Air Act
  d. 28-hour day

2. _____ is the level of inventory that minimizes the total inventory holding costs and ordering costs. The framework used to determine this order quantity is also known as Wilson _____ Model. The model was developed by F. W. Harris in 1913.
  a. Anti-leadership
  b. Effective executive
  c. Economic order quantity
  d. Event management

3. _____ is a concept that aims to enhance supply chain integration by supporting and assisting joint practices. _____ seeks cooperative management of inventory through joint visibility and replenishment of products throughout the supply chain. Information shared between suppliers and retailers aids in planning and satisfying customer demands through a supportive system of shared information.
  a. Timesheets
  b. Collaborative Planning, Forecasting and Replenishment
  c. Groups decision making
  d. Career portfolios

4. Procter is a surname, and may also refer to:

   - Bryan Waller Procter (pseud. Barry Cornwall), English poet
   - Goodwin Procter, American law firm
   - _____, consumer products multinational

   a. Downstream
   b. Strict liability
   c. Master and Servant Acts
   d. Procter ' Gamble

5. The _____ is a financial term defined as a company's operating expenses as a percentage of revenue. This financial ratio is most commonly used for industries such as railroads which require a large percentage of revenues to maintain operations. In railroading, an _____ of 80 or lower is considered desirable.
   a. AAAI
   b. A Stake in the Outcome
   c. Operating ratio
   d. A4e

Chapter 9. Capacity Decisions

6. In microeconomics, industrial organization is the field which describes the behavior of firms in the marketplace with regard to production, pricing, employment and other decisions. _____ in this field range from classical issues such as opportunity cost to neoclassical concepts such as factors of production.

- Production theory basics
    - production efficiency
    - factors of production
    - total, average, and marginal product curves
    - marginal productivity
    - isoquants ' isocosts
    - the marginal rate of technical substitution
- Economic rent
    - classical factor rents
    - Paretian factor rents
- Production possibility frontier
    - what products are possible given a set of resources
    - the trade-off between producing one product rather than another
    - the marginal rate of transformation
- Production function
    - inputs
    - diminishing returns to inputs
    - the stages of production
    - shifts in a production function
- Cost theory
    - the different types of costs
        - opportunity cost
        - accounting cost or historical costs
        - transaction cost
        - sunk cost
        - marginal cost
    - the isocost line
- Cost-of-production theory of value
- Long-run cost and production functions
    - long-run average cost
    - long-run production function and efficiency
    - returns to scale and isoclines
    - minimum efficient scale
    - plant capacity
- Economies of density
- Economies of scale
    - the efficiency consequences of increasing or decreasing the level of production
- Economies of scope
    - the efficiency consequences of increasing or decreasing the number of different types of products produced, promoted, and distributed
- Optimum factor allocation
    - output elasticity of factor costs
    - marginal revenue product
    - marginal resource cost
- Pricing
    - various aspects of the pricing decision
- Transfer pricing
    - selling within a multi-divisional company
- Joint product pricing
    - price setting when two products are linked
- Price discrimination

- - different prices to different buyers
  - types of price discrimination
  - yield management
- Price skimming
  - price discrimination over time
- Two part tariffs
  - charging a price composed of two parts, usually an initial fee and an ongoing fee
- Price points
  - the effects of a non-linear demand curve on pricing
- Cost-plus pricing
  - a markup is applied to a cost term in order to calculate price
  - cost-plus pricing with elasticity considerations
  - cost plus pricing is often used along with break even analysis
- Rate of return pricing
  - calculate price based on the required rate of return on investment, or rate of return on sales
- Profit maximization
  - determining the optimum price and quantity
  - the totals approach
  - marginal approach of production

a. Markup
b. Pricing
c. Price floor
d. Topics

7. _____ refers to increasing the spiritual, political, social or economic strength of individuals and communities. It often involves the empowered developing confidence in their own capacities.

The term Human _____ covers a vast landscape of meanings, interpretations, definitions and disciplines ranging from psychology and philosophy to the highly commercialized Self-Help industry and Motivational sciences.

a. A Stake in the Outcome
b. Empowerment
c. AAAI
d. A4e

8. _____, commonly known as e-commerce, consists of the buying and selling of products or services over electronic systems such as the Internet and other computer networks. The amount of trade conducted electronically has grown extraordinarily with widespread Internet usage. The use of commerce is conducted in this way, spurring and drawing on innovations in electronic funds transfer, supply chain management, Internet marketing, online transaction processing, electronic data interchange (EDI), inventory management systems, and automated data collection systems.
a. Online shopping
b. A Stake in the Outcome
c. A4e
d. Electronic Commerce

9. _____ is a strategic planning method used to evaluate the Strengths, Weaknesses, Opportunities, and Threats involved in a project or in a business venture. It involves specifying the objective of the business venture or project and identifying the internal and external factors that are favorable and unfavorable to achieving that objective. The technique is credited to Albert Humphrey, who led a convention at Stanford University in the 1960s and 1970s using data from Fortune 500 companies.
a. Market share
b. SWOT analysis
c. Corporate image
d. Marketing

10. _____ is an advertisement in which a particular product specifically mentions a competitor by name for the express purpose of showing why the competitor is inferior to the product naming it.

This should not be confused with parody advertisements, where a fictional product is being advertised for the purpose of poking fun at the particular advertisement, nor should it be confused with the use of a coined brand name for the purpose of comparing the product without actually naming an actual competitor. ('Wikipedia tastes better and is less filling than the Encyclopedia Galactica.')

In the 1980s, during what has been referred to as the cola wars, soft-drink manufacturer Pepsi ran a series of advertisements where people, caught on hidden camera, in a blind taste test, chose Pepsi over rival Coca-Cola.

   a. 33 Strategies of War
   b. 1990 Clean Air Act
   c. Comparative advertising
   d. 28-hour day

11. _____ is, in very basic words, a position a firm occupies against its competitors.

According to Michael Porter, the three methods for creating a sustainable _____ are through:

1. Cost leadership

2. Differentiation

3. Focus (economics)

   a. 1990 Clean Air Act
   b. Theory Z
   c. 28-hour day
   d. Competitive advantage

12. The _____ is a trilateral trade bloc in North America created by the governments of the United States, Canada, and Mexico. The agreement creating the trade bloc came into force on January 1, 1994. It superseded the Canada-United States Free Trade Agreement between the U.S. and Canada.
   a. Trade union
   b. North American Free Trade Agreement
   c. Business war game
   d. Career portfolios

13. _____, in microeconomics, are the cost advantages that a business obtains due to expansion. They are factors that cause a producer's average cost per unit to fall as scale is increased. _____ is a long run concept and refers to reductions in unit cost as the size of a facility, or scale, increases.

   a. A Stake in the Outcome
   b. A4e
   c. Economies of scale
   d. Economies of scope

Chapter 10. Facility Location in a Global Environment

1. _____ is a branch of operations research concerning itself with mathematical modeling and solution of problems concerning the placement of facilities in order to minimize transportation costs, avoid placing hazardous materials near housing, outperform competitors' facilities, etc.

A simple _____ problem is the Fermat-Weber problem, in which a single facility is to be placed, with the only optimization criterion being the minimization of the sum of distances from a given set of point sites. More complex problems considered in this discipline include the placement of multiple facilities, constraints on the locations of facilities, and more complex optimization criteria.

   a. Multiscale decision making
   b. 1990 Clean Air Act
   c. 28-hour day
   d. Facility location

2. Procter is a surname, and may also refer to:

   - Bryan Waller Procter (pseud. Barry Cornwall), English poet
   - Goodwin Procter, American law firm
   - _____, consumer products multinational

   a. Strict liability
   b. Procter ' Gamble
   c. Downstream
   d. Master and Servant Acts

3. _____ is an advertisement in which a particular product specifically mentions a competitor by name for the express purpose of showing why the competitor is inferior to the product naming it.

This should not be confused with parody advertisements, where a fictional product is being advertised for the purpose of poking fun at the particular advertisement, nor should it be confused with the use of a coined brand name for the purpose of comparing the product without actually naming an actual competitor. ('Wikipedia tastes better and is less filling than the Encyclopedia Galactica.')

In the 1980s, during what has been referred to as the cola wars, soft-drink manufacturer Pepsi ran a series of advertisements where people, caught on hidden camera, in a blind taste test, chose Pepsi over rival Coca-Cola.

Chapter 10. Facility Location in a Global Environment

a. 33 Strategies of War
b. 28-hour day
c. 1990 Clean Air Act
d. Comparative advertising

4. _____ is a concept that aims to enhance supply chain integration by supporting and assisting joint practices. _____ seeks cooperative management of inventory through joint visibility and replenishment of products throughout the supply chain. Information shared between suppliers and retailers aids in planning and satisfying customer demands through a supportive system of shared information.
   a. Career portfolios
   b. Timesheets
   c. Collaborative Planning, Forecasting and Replenishment
   d. Groups decision making

5. In economics, business, retail, and accounting, a _____ is the value of money that has been used up to produce something, and hence is not available for use anymore. In economics, a _____ is an alternative that is given up as a result of a decision. In business, the _____ may be one of acquisition, in which case the amount of money expended to acquire it is counted as _____.
   a. Fixed costs
   b. Cost
   c. Cost allocation
   d. Cost overrun

6. In economics, and cost accounting, _____ describes the total economic cost of production and is made up of variable costs, which vary according to the quantity of a good produced and include inputs such as labor and raw materials, plus fixed costs, which are independent of the quantity of a good produced and include inputs (capital) that cannot be varied in the short term, such as buildings and machinery. _____ in economics includes the total opportunity cost of each factor of production in addition to fixed and variable costs.

The rate at which _____ changes as the amount produced changes is called marginal cost.

   a. 1990 Clean Air Act
   b. 28-hour day
   c. 33 Strategies of War
   d. Total cost

7. The _____ is a trilateral trade bloc in North America created by the governments of the United States, Canada, and Mexico. The agreement creating the trade bloc came into force on January 1, 1994. It superseded the Canada-United States Free Trade Agreement between the U.S. and Canada.
   a. Career portfolios
   b. North American Free Trade Agreement
   c. Trade union
   d. Business war game

8. In economics and sociology, an _____ is any factor (financial or non-financial) that enables or motivates a particular course of action, or counts as a reason for preferring one choice to the alternatives. It is an expectation that encourages people to behave in a certain way. Since human beings are purposeful creatures, the study of _____ structures is central to the study of all economic activity (both in terms of individual decision-making and in terms of co-operation and competition within a larger institutional structure.)
   a. A4e
   b. A Stake in the Outcome
   c. AAAI
   d. Incentive

9. The _____, widely known as ISO , is an international-standard-setting body composed of representatives from various national standards organizations. Founded on 23 February 1947, the organization promulgates worldwide proprietary industrial and commercial standards. It is headquartered in Geneva, Switzerland.
   a. A4e
   b. A Stake in the Outcome
   c. International Organization for Standardization
   d. AAAI

10. In statistics, _____ refers to techniques for the modeling and analysis of numerical data consisting of values of a dependent variable and of one or more independent variables The dependent variable in the regression equation is modeled as a function of the independent variables, corresponding parameters, and an error term. The error term is treated as a random variable and represents unexplained variation in the dependent variable.
    a. Stepwise regression
    b. Trend analysis
    c. Least squares
    d. Regression analysis

11. _____ is the body of laws, administrative rulings, and precedents which address the legal rights of, and restrictions on, working people and their organizations. As such, it mediates many aspects of the relationship between trade unions, employers and employees. In Canada, employment laws related to unionized workplaces are differentiated from those relating to particular individuals.

   a. Shift work
   b. Four-day week
   c. Labor law
   d. Trade union

12. An _____ is the negative aspects of human activity on the biophysical environment. Environmentalism, a social and environmental movement that started in the 1960s, focuses on addressing _____s through advocacy, education and activism.

Major current _____s are climate change, pollution and resource depletion.

   a. AAAI
   b. Environmental issue
   c. A Stake in the Outcome
   d. A4e

Chapter 11. Facility Layout

1. In probability theory, a probability distribution is called _____ if its cumulative distribution function is _____. This is equivalent to saying that for random variables X with the distribution in question, Pr[X = a] = 0 for all real numbers a, i.e.: the probability that X attains the value a is zero, for any number a. If the distribution of X is _____ then X is called a _____ random variable.
    a. Decision tree pruning
    b. Pay Band
    c. Connectionist expert systems
    d. Continuous

2. _____ is an overall management philosophy introduced by Dr. Eliyahu M. Goldratt in his 1984 book titled The Goal, that is geared to help organizations continually achieve their goal. The title comes from the contention that any manageable system is limited in achieving more of its goal by a very small number of constraints, and that there is always at least one constraint. The _____ process seeks to identify the constraint and restructure the rest of the organization around it, through the use of the Five Focusing Steps.
    a. Six Sigma
    b. Takt time
    c. Production line
    d. Theory of constraints

3. An _____ is a manufacturing process in which parts (usually interchangeable parts) are added to a product in a sequential manner using optimally planned logistics to create a finished product much faster than with handcrafting-type methods. The _____ developed by Ford Motor Company between 1908 and 1915 made _____s famous in the following decade through the social ramifications of mass production, such as the affordability of the Ford Model T and the introduction of high wages for Ford workers. However, the various preconditions for the development at Ford stretched far back into the 19th century, from the gradual realization of the dream of interchangeability, to the concept of reinventing workflow and job descriptions using analytical methods.
    a. A4e
    b. AAAI
    c. A Stake in the Outcome
    d. Assembly line

4. _____ is an advertisement in which a particular product specifically mentions a competitor by name for the express purpose of showing why the competitor is inferior to the product naming it.

This should not be confused with parody advertisements, where a fictional product is being advertised for the purpose of poking fun at the particular advertisement, nor should it be confused with the use of a coined brand name for the purpose of comparing the product without actually naming an actual competitor. ('Wikipedia tastes better and is less filling than the Encyclopedia Galactica.')

In the 1980s, during what has been referred to as the cola wars, soft-drink manufacturer Pepsi ran a series of advertisements where people, caught on hidden camera, in a blind taste test, chose Pepsi over rival Coca-Cola.

a. 33 Strategies of War
b. 28-hour day
c. 1990 Clean Air Act
d. Comparative advertising

5. Procter is a surname, and may also refer to:

- Bryan Waller Procter (pseud. Barry Cornwall), English poet
- Goodwin Procter, American law firm
- _____, consumer products multinational

a. Procter ' Gamble
b. Master and Servant Acts
c. Strict liability
d. Downstream

Chapter 11. Facility Layout

6. In microeconomics, industrial organization is the field which describes the behavior of firms in the marketplace with regard to production, pricing, employment and other decisions. _____ in this field range from classical issues such as opportunity cost to neoclassical concepts such as factors of production.

- Production theory basics
    - production efficiency
    - factors of production
    - total, average, and marginal product curves
    - marginal productivity
    - isoquants ' isocosts
    - the marginal rate of technical substitution
- Economic rent
    - classical factor rents
    - Paretian factor rents
- Production possibility frontier
    - what products are possible given a set of resources
    - the trade-off between producing one product rather than another
    - the marginal rate of transformation
- Production function
    - inputs
    - diminishing returns to inputs
    - the stages of production
    - shifts in a production function
- Cost theory
    - the different types of costs
        - opportunity cost
        - accounting cost or historical costs
        - transaction cost
        - sunk cost
        - marginal cost
    - the isocost line
- Cost-of-production theory of value
- Long-run cost and production functions
    - long-run average cost
    - long-run production function and efficiency
    - returns to scale and isoclines
    - minimum efficient scale
    - plant capacity
- Economies of density
- Economies of scale
    - the efficiency consequences of increasing or decreasing the level of production
- Economies of scope
    - the efficiency consequences of increasing or decreasing the number of different types of products produced, promoted, and distributed
- Optimum factor allocation
    - output elasticity of factor costs
    - marginal revenue product
    - marginal resource cost
- Pricing
    - various aspects of the pricing decision
- Transfer pricing
    - selling within a multi-divisional company
- Joint product pricing
    - price setting when two products are linked
- Price discrimination

- - - different prices to different buyers
    - types of price discrimination
    - yield management
- Price skimming
  - price discrimination over time
- Two part tariffs
  - charging a price composed of two parts, usually an initial fee and an ongoing fee
- Price points
  - the effects of a non-linear demand curve on pricing
- Cost-plus pricing
  - a markup is applied to a cost term in order to calculate price
  - cost-plus pricing with elasticity considerations
  - cost plus pricing is often used along with break even analysis
- Rate of return pricing
  - calculate price based on the required rate of return on investment, or rate of return on sales
- Profit maximization
  - determining the optimum price and quantity
  - the totals approach
  - marginal approach of production

a. Pricing
b. Markup
c. Price floor
d. Topics

7. _____ is a concept that aims to enhance supply chain integration by supporting and assisting joint practices. _____ seeks cooperative management of inventory through joint visibility and replenishment of products throughout the supply chain. Information shared between suppliers and retailers aids in planning and satisfying customer demands through a supportive system of shared information.

a. Groups decision making
b. Timesheets
c. Career portfolios
d. Collaborative Planning, Forecasting and Replenishment

8. _____ refers to increasing the spiritual, political, social or economic strength of individuals and communities. It often involves the empowered developing confidence in their own capacities.

The term Human _____ covers a vast landscape of meanings, interpretations, definitions and disciplines ranging from psychology and philosophy to the highly commercialized Self-Help industry and Motivational sciences.

a. A Stake in the Outcome
b. AAAI
c. A4e
d. Empowerment

9. The field of _____ looks at the relationship between management and workers, particularly groups of workers represented by a union.

_____ is an important factor in analyzing 'varieties of capitalism', such as neocorporatism, social democracy, and neoliberalism

a. Informal organization
b. Organizational effectiveness
c. Industrial relations
d. Overtime

10. The _____ of 1938 (_____, ch. 676, 52 Stat. 1060, June 25, 1938, 29 U.S.C. ch.8), also called the Wages and Hours Bill, is United States federal law that applies to employees engaged in interstate commerce or employed by an enterprise engaged in commerce or in the production of goods for commerce, unless the employer can claim an exemption from coverage. The _____ established a national minimum wage, guaranteed time and a half for overtime in certain jobs, and prohibited most employment of minors in 'oppressive child labor,' a term defined in the statute.

   a. Joint venture
   b. Family and Medical Leave Act of 1993
   c. Fair Labor Standards Act
   d. Board of directors

11. _____ are conventions, treaties and recommendations designed to eliminate unjust and inhumane labour practices. The primary inernational agency charged with developing such standards is the International Labour Organization (ILO.) Established in 1919, the ILO advocates international standards as essential for the eradication of labour conditions involving 'injustice, hardship and privation'.

   a. Anaconda Copper
   b. Airbus SAS
   c. Airbus Industrie
   d. International labour standards

12. _____ is a strategic planning method used to evaluate the Strengths, Weaknesses, Opportunities, and Threats involved in a project or in a business venture. It involves specifying the objective of the business venture or project and identifying the internal and external factors that are favorable and unfavorable to achieving that objective. The technique is credited to Albert Humphrey, who led a convention at Stanford University in the 1960s and 1970s using data from Fortune 500 companies.

   a. Corporate image
   b. Marketing
   c. Market share
   d. SWOT analysis

13. _____ are statistical methods developed by Genichi Taguchi to improve the quality of manufactured goods, and more recently also applied to biotechnology, marketing and advertising. Professional statisticians have welcomed the goals and improvements brought about by _____, particularly by Taguchi's development of designs for studying variation, but have criticized the inefficiency of some of Taguchi's proposals.

Taguchi's work includes three principal contributions to statistics:

1. Taguchi loss function;
2. The philosophy of off-line quality control; and
3. Innovations in the design of experiments.

Traditionally, statistical methods have relied on mean-unbiased estimators of treatment effects: Under the conditions of the Gauss-Markov theorem, least squares estimators have minimum variance among all mean-unbiased estimators. The emphasis on comparisons of means also draws (limiting) comfort from the law of large numbers, according to which the sample means converge to the true mean.

a. 28-hour day
b. Design of experiments
c. Taguchi methods
d. 1990 Clean Air Act

14. _____ is a model for workplace design, and is an integral part of lean manufacturing systems. The goal of lean manufacturing is the aggressive minimisation of waste, called muda, to achieve maximum efficiency of resources. _____, sometimes called cellular or cell production, arranges factory floor labor into semi-autonomous and multi-skilled teams, or work cells, who manufacture complete products or complex components.
a. Productivity
b. Scientific management
c. Remanufacturing
d. Cellular manufacturing

15. A _____ system is a manufacturing system in which there is some amount of flexibility that allows the system to react in the case of changes, whether predicted or unpredicted. This flexibility is generally considered to fall into two categories, which both contain numerous subcategories.

The first category, machine flexibility, covers the system's ability to be changed to produce new product types, and ability to change the order of operations executed on a part. The second category is called routing flexibility, which consists of the ability to use multiple machines to perform the same operation on a part, as well as the system's ability to absorb large-scale changes, such as in volume, capacity, or capability.

a. Homeworkers
b. Manufacturing resource planning
c. Jidoka
d. Flexible manufacturing

16. _____ is a software based production planning and inventory control system used to manage manufacturing processes. Although it is not common nowadays, it is possible to conduct _____ by hand as well.

An _____ system is intended to simultaneously meet three objectives:

- Ensure materials and products are available for production and delivery to customers.
- Maintain the lowest possible level of inventory.
- Plan manufacturing activities, delivery schedules and purchasing activities.

Manufacturing organizations, whatever their products, face the same daily practical problem - that customers want products to be available in a shorter time than it takes to make them. This means that some level of planning is required.

a. Material requirements planning
b. 33 Strategies of War
c. 1990 Clean Air Act
d. 28-hour day

17. _____ are typically small manufacturing operations that handle specialized manufacturing processes such as small customer orders or small batch jobs. _____ typically move on to different jobs (possibly with different customers) when each job is completed. By nature of this type of manufacturing operation, _____ are usually specialized in skill and processes.
a. 1990 Clean Air Act
b. Job shops
c. 33 Strategies of War
d. 28-hour day

18. The function f is called, variously, an _____, cost function, energy function, or energy functional. A feasible solution that minimizes (or maximizes, if that is the goal) the _____ is called an optimal solution.

Generally, when the feasible region or the _____ of the problem does not present convexity, there may be several local minima and maxima, where a local minimum x^* is defined as a point for which there exists some $>\delta > 0$ so that for all x such that

$$\left| x \right| >$$

the expression

$$\left| x \right| >$$

holds; that is to say, on some region around x* all of the function values are greater than or equal to the value at that point.

a. A4e
b. A Stake in the Outcome
c. AAAI
d. Objective function

19. _____ of the learning curve effect and the closely related experience curve effect express the relationship between equations for experience and efficiency or between efficiency gains and investment in the effort. The experience of 'learning curves' was first observed by the 19th Century German psychologist Hermann Ebbinghaus according to the difficulty of memorizing varying numbers of verbal stimuli, and subsequent learning about the complex processes of learning are discussed in the

.

The rule used for representing the learning curve effect states that the more times a task has been performed, the less time will be required on each subsequent iteration.

a. Models
b. Distribution
c. Point biserial correlation coefficient
d. Spatial Decision Support Systems

20. _____ is, in very basic words, a position a firm occupies against its competitors.

According to Michael Porter, the three methods for creating a sustainable _____ are through:

1. Cost leadership

2. Differentiation

3. Focus (economics)

a. 28-hour day
b. Competitive advantage
c. Theory Z
d. 1990 Clean Air Act

Chapter 12. Aggregate Planning

1. _____ is an operational activity which does an aggregate plan for the production process, in advance of 2 to 18 months, to give an idea to management as to what quantity of materials and other resources are to be procured and when, so that the total cost of operations of the organization is kept to the minimum over that period.

The quantity of outsourcing, subcontracting of items, overtime of labor, numbers to be hired and fired in each period and the amount of inventory to be held in stock and to be backlogged for each period are decided. All of these activities are done within the framework of the company ethics, policies, and long term commitment to the society, community and the country of operation.

   a. Earned value management
   b. A Stake in the Outcome
   c. Earned Schedule
   d. Aggregate planning

2. _____ is an organization's process of defining its strategy and making decisions on allocating its resources to pursue this strategy, including its capital and people. Various business analysis techniques can be used in _____, including SWOT analysis (Strengths, Weaknesses, Opportunities, and Threats) and PEST analysis (Political, Economic, Social, and Technological analysis) or STEER analysis involving Socio-cultural, Technological, Economic, Ecological, and Regulatory factors and EPISTEL (Environment, Political, Informatic, Social, Technological, Economic and Legal)

_____ is the formal consideration of an organization's future course. All _____ deals with at least one of three key questions:

   1. 'What do we do?'
   2. 'For whom do we do it?'
   3. 'How do we excel?'

In business _____, the third question is better phrased 'How can we beat or avoid competition?'. (Bradford and Duncan, page 1.)

   a. 1990 Clean Air Act
   b. 33 Strategies of War
   c. 28-hour day
   d. Strategic planning

3. _____ is a concept that aims to enhance supply chain integration by supporting and assisting joint practices. _____ seeks cooperative management of inventory through joint visibility and replenishment of products throughout the supply chain. Information shared between suppliers and retailers aids in planning and satisfying customer demands through a supportive system of shared information.

a. Timesheets
b. Career portfolios
c. Groups decision making
d. Collaborative Planning, Forecasting and Replenishment

4. The _____ is a systematic, interactive forecasting method which relies on a panel of independent experts. The carefully selected experts answer questionnaires in two or more rounds. After each round, a facilitator provides an anonymous summary of the experts' forecasts from the previous round as well as the reasons they provided for their judgments.
   a. Learning organization
   b. Quality function deployment
   c. Hoshin Kanri
   d. Delphi method

5. _____ ('Plan-Do-Check-Act') is an iterative four-step problem-solving process typically used in business process improvement. It is also known as the Deming Cycle, Shewhart cycle, Deming Wheel, or Plan-Do-Study-Act.

   _____ was made popular by Dr. W. Edwards Deming, who is considered by many to be the father of modern quality control; however it was always referred to by him as the Shewhart cycle. Later in Deming's career, he modified _____ to Plan, Do, Study, Act (PDSA) so as to better describe his recommendations.

   a. Decentralization
   b. Management by exception
   c. Management team
   d. PDCA

6. In economics, _____ is the desire to own something and the ability to pay for it. The term _____ signifies the ability or the willingness to buy a particular commodity at a given point of time.
   a. Demand
   b. 1990 Clean Air Act
   c. 28-hour day
   d. 33 Strategies of War

7. _____ is an integrated communications-based process through which individuals and communities discover that existing and newly-identified needs and wants may be satisfied by the products and services of others.

Chapter 12. Aggregate Planning 87

_____ is defined by the American _____ Association as the activity, set of institutions, and processes for creating, communicating, delivering, and exchanging offerings that have value for customers, clients, partners, and society at large. The term developed from the original meaning which referred literally to going to market, as in shopping, or going to a market to buy or sell goods or services.

a. Market development
b. Marketing
c. Customer relationship management
d. Disruptive technology

8. In economics, business, retail, and accounting, a _____ is the value of money that has been used up to produce something, and hence is not available for use anymore. In economics, a _____ is an alternative that is given up as a result of a decision. In business, the _____ may be one of acquisition, in which case the amount of money expended to acquire it is counted as _____.

a. Cost allocation
b. Fixed costs
c. Cost overrun
d. Cost

9. Business-to-consumer describes activities of businesses serving end consumers with products and/or services.

An example of a _____ transaction would be a person buying a pair of shoes from a retailer. The transactions that led to the shoes being available for purchase, that is the purchase of the leather, laces, rubber, etc.

a. Green marketing
b. PEST analysis
c. B2C
d. Market environment

10. _____ is an advertisement in which a particular product specifically mentions a competitor by name for the express purpose of showing why the competitor is inferior to the product naming it.

This should not be confused with parody advertisements, where a fictional product is being advertised for the purpose of poking fun at the particular advertisement, nor should it be confused with the use of a coined brand name for the purpose of comparing the product without actually naming an actual competitor. ('Wikipedia tastes better and is less filling than the Encyclopedia Galactica.')

In the 1980s, during what has been referred to as the cola wars, soft-drink manufacturer Pepsi ran a series of advertisements where people, caught on hidden camera, in a blind taste test, chose Pepsi over rival Coca-Cola.

a. 33 Strategies of War
b. 28-hour day
c. 1990 Clean Air Act
d. Comparative advertising

11. _____ is the process of understanding, anticipating and influencing consumer behavior in order to maximize revenue or profits from a fixed, perishable resource This process was first discovered by Dr. Matt H. Keller. The challenge is to sell the right resources to the right customer at the right time for the right price.
   a. Yield management
   b. Business networking
   c. Business model design
   d. Gap analysis

12. _____ is a method of planning and managing projects that puts the main emphasis on the resources required to execute project tasks. It was developed by Eliyahu M. Goldratt. This is in contrast to the more traditional Critical Path and PERT methods, which emphasize task order and rigid scheduling. A Critical Chain project network will tend to keep the resources levelly loaded, but will require them to be flexible in their start times and to quickly switch between tasks and task chains to keep the whole project on schedule.
   a. Project engineer
   b. Project management office
   c. Critical Chain Project Management
   d. Precedence diagram

13. The _____, widely known as ISO , is an international-standard-setting body composed of representatives from various national standards organizations. Founded on 23 February 1947, the organization promulgates worldwide proprietary industrial and commercial standards. It is headquartered in Geneva, Switzerland.
   a. A Stake in the Outcome
   b. A4e
   c. AAAI
   d. International Organization for Standardization

Chapter 12. Aggregate Planning

14. _____ is subcontracting a process, such as product design or manufacturing, to a third-party company. The decision to outsource is often made in the interest of lowering cost or making better use of time and energy costs, redirecting or conserving energy directed at the competencies of a particular business, or to make more efficient use of land, labor, capital, (information) technology and resources. _____ became part of the business lexicon during the 1980s.
    a. Unemployment insurance
    b. Outsourcing
    c. Opinion leadership
    d. Operant conditioning

15. _____ is the amount of time someone works beyond normal working hours. Normal hours may be determined in several ways:

    - by custom (what is considered healthy or reasonable by society),
    - by practices of a given trade or profession,
    - by legislation,
    - by agreement between employers and workers or their representatives.

    Most nations have _____ laws designed to dissuade or prevent employers from forcing their employees to work excessively long hours. These laws may take into account other considerations than the humanitarian, such as increasing the overall level of employment in the economy. One common approach to regulating _____ is to require employers to pay workers at a higher hourly rate for _____ work.

    a. Industrial relations
    b. Organizational effectiveness
    c. Organizational structure
    d. Overtime

16. The _____ is the labour pool in employment. It is generally used to describe those working for a single company or industry, but can also apply to a geographic region like a city, country, state, etc. The term generally excludes the employers or management, and implies those involved in manual labour.
    a. Division of labour
    b. Pink-collar worker
    c. Work-life balance
    d. Workforce

17. The _____ is a trilateral trade bloc in North America created by the governments of the United States, Canada, and Mexico. The agreement creating the trade bloc came into force on January 1, 1994. It superseded the Canada-United States Free Trade Agreement between the U.S. and Canada.

a. Business war game
b. Trade union
c. Career portfolios
d. North American Free Trade Agreement

Chapter 13. Planning for Material and Resource Requirements

1. A _____ is a plan for production, staffing, inventory, etc. It is usually linked to manufacturing where the plan indicates when and how much of each product will be demanded. This plan quantifies significant processes, parts, and other resources in order to optimize production, to identify bottlenecks, and to anticipate needs and completed goods.
   a. Remanufacturing
   b. Value engineering
   c. Piecework
   d. Master production schedule

2. _____ is a concept that aims to enhance supply chain integration by supporting and assisting joint practices. _____ seeks cooperative management of inventory through joint visibility and replenishment of products throughout the supply chain. Information shared between suppliers and retailers aids in planning and satisfying customer demands through a supportive system of shared information.
   a. Timesheets
   b. Groups decision making
   c. Collaborative Planning, Forecasting and Replenishment
   d. Career portfolios

3. _____ is a business function that provides a response to customer order enquiries, based on resource availability. It generates available quantities of the requested product, and delivery due dates. Therefore, _____ supports order promising and fulfillment, aiming to manage demand and match it to production plans.
   a. Available-to-promise
   b. A4e
   c. AAAI
   d. A Stake in the Outcome

4. _____ is an advertisement in which a particular product specifically mentions a competitor by name for the express purpose of showing why the competitor is inferior to the product naming it.

This should not be confused with parody advertisements, where a fictional product is being advertised for the purpose of poking fun at the particular advertisement, nor should it be confused with the use of a coined brand name for the purpose of comparing the product without actually naming an actual competitor. ('Wikipedia tastes better and is less filling than the Encyclopedia Galactica.')

In the 1980s, during what has been referred to as the cola wars, soft-drink manufacturer Pepsi ran a series of advertisements where people, caught on hidden camera, in a blind taste test, chose Pepsi over rival Coca-Cola.

Chapter 13. Planning for Material and Resource Requirements

   a. 28-hour day
   b. 1990 Clean Air Act
   c. 33 Strategies of War
   d. Comparative advertising

5. The _____ is a systematic, interactive forecasting method which relies on a panel of independent experts. The carefully selected experts answer questionnaires in two or more rounds. After each round, a facilitator provides an anonymous summary of the experts' forecasts from the previous round as well as the reasons they provided for their judgments.
   a. Quality function deployment
   b. Hoshin Kanri
   c. Learning organization
   d. Delphi method

6. _____ is the process of determining the production capacity needed by an organization to meet changing demands for its products. In the context of _____, 'capacity' is the maximum amount of work that an organization is capable of completing in a given period of time.

A discrepancy between the capacity of an organization and the demands of its customers results in inefficiency, either in under-utilized resources or unfulfilled customers.

   a. Remanufacturing
   b. Scientific management
   c. Productivity
   d. Capacity planning

7. In economics, _____ is the desire to own something and the ability to pay for it. The term _____ signifies the ability or the willingness to buy a particular commodity at a given point of time.
   a. 33 Strategies of War
   b. Demand
   c. 1990 Clean Air Act
   d. 28-hour day

8. In economics, _____' is the art or science of controlling economic demand to avoid a recession. In natural resources management and environmental policy more generally, it refers to policies to control consumer demand for environmentally sensitive or harmful goods such as water and energy. Within manufacturing firms the term is used to describe the activities of demand forecasting, planning and order fulfillment.

a. 33 Strategies of War
b. Demand management
c. 1990 Clean Air Act
d. 28-hour day

9. _____ is a process of planning and controlling the performance or execution of any type of activity, such as:

- a project (project _____) or
- a process (process _____, sometimes referred to as the process performance measurement and management system.)

Organization's senior management is responsible for carrying out its _____.

a. Management process
b. Work design
c. Participatory management
d. Human Relations Movement

10. _____ is one of the managerial functions like planning, organizing, staffing and directing. It is an important function because it helps to check the errors and to take the corrective action so that deviation from standards are minimized and stated goals of the organization are achieved in desired manner.According to modern concepts, _____ is a foreseeing action whereas earlier concept of _____ was used only when errors were detected. _____ in management means setting standards, measuring actual performance and taking corrective action.

a. Decision tree pruning
b. Turnover
c. Schedule of reinforcement
d. Control

11. _____ is a software based production planning and inventory control system used to manage manufacturing processes. Although it is not common nowadays, it is possible to conduct _____ by hand as well.

An _____ system is intended to simultaneously meet three objectives:

- Ensure materials and products are available for production and delivery to customers.
- Maintain the lowest possible level of inventory.
- Plan manufacturing activities, delivery schedules and purchasing activities.

Manufacturing organizations, whatever their products, face the same daily practical problem - that customers want products to be available in a shorter time than it takes to make them. This means that some level of planning is required.

a. 28-hour day
b. 1990 Clean Air Act
c. Material requirements planning
d. 33 Strategies of War

12. _____ ('Plan-Do-Check-Act') is an iterative four-step problem-solving process typically used in business process improvement. It is also known as the Deming Cycle, Shewhart cycle, Deming Wheel, or Plan-Do-Study-Act.

_____ was made popular by Dr. W. Edwards Deming, who is considered by many to be the father of modern quality control; however it was always referred to by him as the Shewhart cycle. Later in Deming's career, he modified _____ to Plan, Do, Study, Act (PDSA) so as to better describe his recommendations.

a. Management by exception
b. Decentralization
c. Management team
d. PDCA

13. _____ is a list of the raw materials, sub-assemblies, intermediate assemblies, sub-components, components, parts and the quantities of each needed to manufacture an end item (final product).
a. Piece rate
b. Methods-time measurement
c. Scientific management
d. Bill of materials

14. A _____ is a decision support tool that uses a tree-like graph or model of decisions and their possible consequences, including chance event outcomes, resource costs, and utility. _____s are commonly used in operations research, specifically in decision analysis, to help identify a strategy most likely to reach a goal. Another use of _____s is as a descriptive means for calculating conditional probabilities.
a. Decision tree
b. 1990 Clean Air Act
c. 33 Strategies of War
d. 28-hour day

15. The _____, widely known as ISO , is an international-standard-setting body composed of representatives from various national standards organizations. Founded on 23 February 1947, the organization promulgates worldwide proprietary industrial and commercial standards. It is headquartered in Geneva, Switzerland.

Chapter 13. Planning for Material and Resource Requirements

a. A4e
b. AAAI
c. A Stake in the Outcome
d. International Organization for Standardization

16. In statistics, _____ refers to techniques for the modeling and analysis of numerical data consisting of values of a dependent variable and of one or more independent variables The dependent variable in the regression equation is modeled as a function of the independent variables, corresponding parameters, and an error term. The error term is treated as a random variable and represents unexplained variation in the dependent variable.
    a. Stepwise regression
    b. Regression analysis
    c. Least squares
    d. Trend analysis

17. _____ is a method of planning and managing projects that puts the main emphasis on the resources required to execute project tasks. It was developed by Eliyahu M. Goldratt. This is in contrast to the more traditional Critical Path and PERT methods, which emphasize task order and rigid scheduling. A Critical Chain project network will tend to keep the resources levelly loaded, but will require them to be flexible in their start times and to quickly switch between tasks and task chains to keep the whole project on schedule.
    a. Project management office
    b. Precedence diagram
    c. Critical Chain Project Management
    d. Project engineer

18. A _____ is a commercial document issued by a buyer to a seller, indicating types, quantities, and agreed prices for products or services the seller will provide to the buyer. Sending a _____ to a supplier constitutes a legal offer to buy products or services. Acceptance of a _____ by a seller usually forms a one-off contract between the buyer and seller, so no contract exists until the _____ is accepted.
    a. 28-hour day
    b. 33 Strategies of War
    c. 1990 Clean Air Act
    d. Purchase order

Chapter 13. Planning for Material and Resource Requirements

19. _____ is defined by APICS as a method for the effective planning of all resources of a manufacturing company. Ideally, it addresses operational planning in units, financial planning in dollars, and has a simulation capability to answer 'what-if' questions and extension of closed-loop _____. Manufacturing resource planning (or Manufacturing resource planning2) - Around 1980, over-frequent changes in sales forecasts, entailing continual readjustments in production, as well as the unsuitability of the parameters fixed by the system, led _____ (Material Requirement Planning) to evolve into a new concept : _____ (e.g. _____ 2)

This is not exclusively a software function, but a marriage of people skills, dedication to data base accuracy, and computer resources.

   a. MRP II
   b. Jidoka
   c. Manufacturing resource planning
   d. Homeworkers

20. _____ is an organization's process of defining its strategy and making decisions on allocating its resources to pursue this strategy, including its capital and people. Various business analysis techniques can be used in _____, including SWOT analysis (Strengths, Weaknesses, Opportunities, and Threats) and PEST analysis (Political, Economic, Social, and Technological analysis) or STEER analysis involving Socio-cultural, Technological, Economic, Ecological, and Regulatory factors and EPISTEL (Environment, Political, Informatic, Social, Technological, Economic and Legal)

_____ is the formal consideration of an organization's future course. All _____ deals with at least one of three key questions:

   1. 'What do we do?'
   2. 'For whom do we do it?'
   3. 'How do we excel?'

In business _____, the third question is better phrased 'How can we beat or avoid competition?'. (Bradford and Duncan, page 1.)

   a. 28-hour day
   b. 1990 Clean Air Act
   c. 33 Strategies of War
   d. Strategic planning

21. Manufacturing Resource Planning (_____) is defined by APICS as a method for the effective planning of all resources of a manufacturing company. Ideally, it addresses operational planning in units, financial planning in dollars, and has a simulation capability to answer 'what-if' questions and extension of closed-loop MRP. Manufacturing Resource Planning (or MRP2) - Around 1980, over-frequent changes in sales forecasts, entailing continual readjustments in production, as well as the unsuitability of the parameters fixed by the system, led MRP (Material Requirement Planning) to evolve into a new concept : Manufacturing Resource Planning (e.g. MRP 2)

Chapter 13. Planning for Material and Resource Requirements

This is not exclusively a software function, but a marriage of people skills, dedication to data base accuracy, and computer resources.

a. MRP II
b. Homeworkers
c. Jidoka
d. Manufacturing resource planning

22. _____ is one of the four elements of marketing mix. An organization or set of organizations (go-betweens) involved in the process of making a product or service available for use or consumption by a consumer or business user.

The other three parts of the marketing mix are product, pricing, and promotion.

a. Distribution
b. Matching theory
c. Job creation programs
d. Missing completely at random

23. _____ is a company-wide computer software system used to manage and coordinate all the resources, information, and functions of a business from shared data stores.

An _____ system has a service-oriented architecture with modular hardware and software units and 'services' that communicate on a local area network. The modular design allows a business to add or reconfigure modules (perhaps from different vendors) while preserving data integrity in one shared database that may be centralized or distributed.

a. AAAI
b. A4e
c. A Stake in the Outcome
d. Enterprise resource planning

Chapter 14. Inventory Management

1. In economics, _____ is the desire to own something and the ability to pay for it. The term _____ signifies the ability or the willingness to buy a particular commodity at a given point of time.
   a. 1990 Clean Air Act
   b. 33 Strategies of War
   c. 28-hour day
   d. Demand

2. A barcode (also bar code) is an optical machine-readable representation of data. Originally, _____ represented data in the widths (lines) and the spacings of parallel lines, and may be referred to as linear or 1D (1 dimensional) barcodes or symbologies. They also come in patterns of squares, dots, hexagons and other geometric patterns within images termed 2D (2 dimensional) matrix codes or symbologies.
   a. Bar codes
   b. 28-hour day
   c. 33 Strategies of War
   d. 1990 Clean Air Act

3. In probability theory, a probability distribution is called _____ if its cumulative distribution function is _____. This is equivalent to saying that for random variables X with the distribution in question, Pr[X = a] = 0 for all real numbers a, i.e.: the probability that X attains the value a is zero, for any number a. If the distribution of X is _____ then X is called a _____ random variable.
   a. Pay Band
   b. Connectionist expert systems
   c. Decision tree pruning
   d. Continuous

4. _____ is a concept that aims to enhance supply chain integration by supporting and assisting joint practices. _____ seeks cooperative management of inventory through joint visibility and replenishment of products throughout the supply chain. Information shared between suppliers and retailers aids in planning and satisfying customer demands through a supportive system of shared information.
   a. Groups decision making
   b. Career portfolios
   c. Timesheets
   d. Collaborative Planning, Forecasting and Replenishment

5. The _____ is an equation that equals the cost of goods sold divided by the average inventory. Average inventory equals beginning inventory plus ending inventory divided by 2.

Chapter 14. Inventory Management

The formula for _____:

$$\boxed{}>$$

The formula for average inventory:

$$\boxed{}>$$

A low turnover rate may point to overstocking, obsolescence, or deficiencies in the product line or marketing effort.

a. A4e
b. Inventory turnover
c. Asset turnover
d. A Stake in the Outcome

6. _____ is one of the Accounting Liquidity ratios, a financial ratio. This ratio measures the number of times, on average, the inventory is sold during the period. Its purpose is to measure the liquidity of the inventory.

a. A4e
b. Inventory
c. A Stake in the Outcome
d. Inventory turnover ratio

7. In a human resources context, _____ or labor _____ is the rate at which an employer gains and loses employees. Simple ways to describe it are 'how long employees tend to stay' or 'the rate of traffic through the revolving door.' _____ is measured for individual companies and for their industry as a whole. If an employer is said to have a high _____ relative to its competitors, it means that employees of that company have a shorter average tenure than those of other companies in the same industry.

a. Ten year occupational employment projection
b. Continuous
c. Turnover
d. Career portfolios

8. The _____ states that, for many events, roughly 80% of the effects come from 20% of the causes. Business management thinker Joseph M. Juran suggested the principle and named it after Italian economist Vilfredo Pareto, who observed that 80% of the land in Italy was owned by 20% of the population. It is a common rule of thumb in business; e.g., '80% of your sales come from 20% of your clients.' Mathematically, where something is shared among a sufficiently large set of participants, there will always be a number k between 50 and 100 such that k% is taken by% of the participants.
   a. Greenfield agreement
   b. Bylaw
   c. Board of directors
   d. Pareto Principle

9. In economics, business, retail, and accounting, a _____ is the value of money that has been used up to produce something, and hence is not available for use anymore. In economics, a _____ is an alternative that is given up as a result of a decision. In business, the _____ may be one of acquisition, in which case the amount of money expended to acquire it is counted as _____.
   a. Cost allocation
   b. Fixed costs
   c. Cost overrun
   d. Cost

10. _____ is the level of inventory that minimizes the total inventory holding costs and ordering costs. The framework used to determine this order quantity is also known as Wilson _____ Model. The model was developed by F. W. Harris in 1913.
    a. Anti-leadership
    b. Effective executive
    c. Event management
    d. Economic order quantity

11. In business management, _____ is money spent to keep and maintain a stock of goods in storage.

The most obvious _____s include rent for the required space; equipment, materials, and labor to operate the space; insurance; security; interest on money invested in the inventory and space, and other direct expenses. Some stored goods become obsolete before they are sold, reducing their contribution to revenue while having no effect on their _____.

   a. Market niche
   b. Holding cost
   c. Choquet integral
   d. Private placement

Chapter 14. Inventory Management

12. _____ is a term used by inventory specialists to describe a level of extra stock that is maintained below the cycle stock to buffer against stockouts. _____ exists to counter uncertainties in supply and demand. _____ is defined as extra units of inventory carried as protection against possible stockouts .(shortfall in raw material or packaging.)
   a. Knowledge worker
   b. Product life cycle
   c. Process automation
   d. Safety stock

13. _____ is an advertisement in which a particular product specifically mentions a competitor by name for the express purpose of showing why the competitor is inferior to the product naming it.

This should not be confused with parody advertisements, where a fictional product is being advertised for the purpose of poking fun at the particular advertisement, nor should it be confused with the use of a coined brand name for the purpose of comparing the product without actually naming an actual competitor. ('Wikipedia tastes better and is less filling than the Encyclopedia Galactica.')

In the 1980s, during what has been referred to as the cola wars, soft-drink manufacturer Pepsi ran a series of advertisements where people, caught on hidden camera, in a blind taste test, chose Pepsi over rival Coca-Cola.

   a. Comparative advertising
   b. 1990 Clean Air Act
   c. 28-hour day
   d. 33 Strategies of War

14. _____ measures the performance of a system. Certain goals are defined and the _____ gives the percentage to which they should be achieved.

Examples

- Percentage of calls answered in a call center.
- Percentage of customers waiting less than a given fixed time.
- Percentage of customers that do not experience a stock out.

_____ is used in supply chain management and in inventory management to measure the performance of inventory systems.

Under stochastic conditions it is unavoidable that in some periods the inventory on hand is not sufficient to deliver the complete demand and, as a consequence, that part of the demand is filled only after an inventory-related waiting time.

a. 33 Strategies of War
b. 28-hour day
c. Service level
d. 1990 Clean Air Act

15. The _____, widely known as ISO , is an international-standard-setting body composed of representatives from various national standards organizations. Founded on 23 February 1947, the organization promulgates worldwide proprietary industrial and commercial standards. It is headquartered in Geneva, Switzerland.
    a. A Stake in the Outcome
    b. A4e
    c. AAAI
    d. International Organization for Standardization

16. In statistics, _____ refers to techniques for the modeling and analysis of numerical data consisting of values of a dependent variable and of one or more independent variables The dependent variable in the regression equation is modeled as a function of the independent variables, corresponding parameters, and an error term. The error term is treated as a random variable and represents unexplained variation in the dependent variable.
    a. Regression analysis
    b. Least squares
    c. Stepwise regression
    d. Trend analysis

1. _____ is an inventory strategy that strives to improve the return on investment of a business by reducing in-process inventory and its associated carrying costs. To meet _____ objectives, the process relies on signals between different points in the process. This means the process is often driven by a series of signals, or Kanban , which tell production when to make the next part. Kanban are usually 'tickets' but can be simple visual signals, such as the presence or absence of a part on a shelf. Implemented correctly, _____ can dramatically improve a manufacturing organization's return on investment, quality, and efficiency.
   a. Just-in-time
   b. 28-hour day
   c. 33 Strategies of War
   d. 1990 Clean Air Act

2. _____ is an organization's process of defining its strategy and making decisions on allocating its resources to pursue this strategy, including its capital and people. Various business analysis techniques can be used in _____, including SWOT analysis (Strengths, Weaknesses, Opportunities, and Threats) and PEST analysis (Political, Economic, Social, and Technological analysis) or STEER analysis involving Socio-cultural, Technological, Economic, Ecological, and Regulatory factors and EPISTEL (Environment, Political, Informatic, Social, Technological, Economic and Legal)

_____ is the formal consideration of an organization's future course. All _____ deals with at least one of three key questions:

   1. 'What do we do?'
   2. 'For whom do we do it?'
   3. 'How do we excel?'

In business _____, the third question is better phrased 'How can we beat or avoid competition?'. (Bradford and Duncan, page 1.)

   a. Strategic planning
   b. 33 Strategies of War
   c. 1990 Clean Air Act
   d. 28-hour day

3. Procter is a surname, and may also refer to:

   - Bryan Waller Procter (pseud. Barry Cornwall), English poet
   - Goodwin Procter, American law firm
   - _____, consumer products multinational

a. Master and Servant Acts
b. Downstream
c. Strict liability
d. Procter ' Gamble

4. In economics, business, retail, and accounting, a _____ is the value of money that has been used up to produce something, and hence is not available for use anymore. In economics, a _____ is an alternative that is given up as a result of a decision. In business, the _____ may be one of acquisition, in which case the amount of money expended to acquire it is counted as _____.
   a. Cost overrun
   b. Fixed costs
   c. Cost allocation
   d. Cost

5. _____ can be considered to have three main components: quality control, quality assurance and quality improvement. _____ is focused not only on product quality, but also the means to achieve it. _____ therefore uses quality assurance and control of processes as well as products to achieve more consistent quality.
   a. Quality management
   b. 28-hour day
   c. Total quality management
   d. 1990 Clean Air Act

6. _____ is a business management strategy aimed at embedding awareness of quality in all organizational processes. _____ has been widely used in manufacturing, education, hospitals, call centers, government, and service industries, as well as NASA space and science programs.

As defined by the International Organization for Standardization (ISO):

'_____ is a management approach for an organization, centered on quality, based on the participation of all its members and aiming at long-term success through customer satisfaction, and benefits to all members of the organization and to society.' ISO 8402:1994

One major aim is to reduce variation from every process so that greater consistency of effort is obtained. (Royse, D., Thyer, B., Padgett D., ' Logan T., 2006)

Chapter 15. Just-in-Time and Theory of Constraints

a. 1990 Clean Air Act
b. Quality management
c. 28-hour day
d. Total quality management

7. _____ is a method of planning and managing projects that puts the main emphasis on the resources required to execute project tasks. It was developed by Eliyahu M. Goldratt. This is in contrast to the more traditional Critical Path and PERT methods, which emphasize task order and rigid scheduling. A Critical Chain project network will tend to keep the resources levelly loaded, but will require them to be flexible in their start times and to quickly switch between tasks and task chains to keep the whole project on schedule.
   a. Critical Chain Project Management
   b. Project engineer
   c. Project management office
   d. Precedence diagram

8. _____ is a concept related to lean and just-in-time (JIT) production. The Japanese word _____ is a common term meaning 'signboard' or 'billboard'. According to Taiichi Ohno, the man credited with developing JIT, _____ is a means through which JIT is achieved.
   a. Trademark
   b. Kanban
   c. Risk management
   d. Succession planning

9. The _____, widely known as ISO , is an international-standard-setting body composed of representatives from various national standards organizations. Founded on 23 February 1947, the organization promulgates worldwide proprietary industrial and commercial standards. It is headquartered in Geneva, Switzerland.
   a. AAAI
   b. A Stake in the Outcome
   c. A4e
   d. International Organization for Standardization

10. _____ refers to increasing the spiritual, political, social or economic strength of individuals and communities. It often involves the empowered developing confidence in their own capacities.

The term Human _____ covers a vast landscape of meanings, interpretations, definitions and disciplines ranging from psychology and philosophy to the highly commercialized Self-Help industry and Motivational sciences.

a. AAAI
b. A Stake in the Outcome
c. A4e
d. Empowerment

11. _____ has the following meanings:

The care and servicing by personnel for the purpose of maintaining equipment and facilities in satisfactory operating condition by providing for systematic inspection, detection, and correction of incipient failures either before they occur or before they develop into major defects.

1. Maintenance, including tests, measurements, adjustments, and parts replacement, performed specifically to prevent faults from occurring.

While _____ is generally considered to be worthwhile, there are risks such as equipment failure or human error involved when performing _____, just as in any maintenance operation. _____ as scheduled overhaul or scheduled replacement provides two of the three proactive failure management policies available to the maintenance engineer. Common methods of determining what _____ failure management policies should be applied are; OEM recommendations, requirements of codes and legislation within a jurisdiction, what an 'expert' thinks ought to be done, or the maintenance that's already done to similar equipment.

a. 28-hour day
b. 33 Strategies of War
c. Preventive maintenance
d. 1990 Clean Air Act

12. _____ ('Plan-Do-Check-Act') is an iterative four-step problem-solving process typically used in business process improvement. It is also known as the Deming Cycle, Shewhart cycle, Deming Wheel, or Plan-Do-Study-Act.

_____ was made popular by Dr. W. Edwards Deming, who is considered by many to be the father of modern quality control; however it was always referred to by him as the Shewhart cycle. Later in Deming's career, he modified _____ to Plan, Do, Study, Act (PDSA) so as to better describe his recommendations.

a. Management team
b. Decentralization
c. Management by exception
d. PDCA

Chapter 15. Just-in-Time and Theory of Constraints

13. _____ are statistical methods developed by Genichi Taguchi to improve the quality of manufactured goods, and more recently also applied to biotechnology, marketing and advertising. Professional statisticians have welcomed the goals and improvements brought about by _____, particularly by Taguchi's development of designs for studying variation, but have criticized the inefficiency of some of Taguchi's proposals.

Taguchi's work includes three principal contributions to statistics:

1. Taguchi loss function;
2. The philosophy of off-line quality control; and
3. Innovations in the design of experiments.

Traditionally, statistical methods have relied on mean-unbiased estimators of treatment effects: Under the conditions of the Gauss-Markov theorem, least squares estimators have minimum variance among all mean-unbiased estimators. The emphasis on comparisons of means also draws (limiting) comfort from the law of large numbers, according to which the sample means converge to the true mean.

a. 1990 Clean Air Act
b. Design of experiments
c. 28-hour day
d. Taguchi methods

14. _____ is a costing model that identifies activities in an organization and assigns the cost of each activity resource to all products and services according to the actual consumption by each: it assigns more indirect costs (overhead) into direct costs.

In this way an organization can establish the true cost of its individual products and services for the purposes of identifying and eliminating those which are unprofitable and lowering the prices of those which are overpriced.

In a business organization, the ABC methodology assigns an organization's resource costs through activities to the products and services provided to its customers.

a. Activity-based costing
b. Indirect costs
c. A4e
d. A Stake in the Outcome

15. Business-to-consumer describes activities of businesses serving end consumers with products and/or services.

An example of a _____ transaction would be a person buying a pair of shoes from a retailer. The transactions that led to the shoes being available for purchase, that is the purchase of the leather, laces, rubber, etc.

a. PEST analysis
b. Market environment
c. B2C
d. Green marketing

16. _____ is an advertisement in which a particular product specifically mentions a competitor by name for the express purpose of showing why the competitor is inferior to the product naming it.

This should not be confused with parody advertisements, where a fictional product is being advertised for the purpose of poking fun at the particular advertisement, nor should it be confused with the use of a coined brand name for the purpose of comparing the product without actually naming an actual competitor. ('Wikipedia tastes better and is less filling than the Encyclopedia Galactica.')

In the 1980s, during what has been referred to as the cola wars, soft-drink manufacturer Pepsi ran a series of advertisements where people, caught on hidden camera, in a blind taste test, chose Pepsi over rival Coca-Cola.

a. 28-hour day
b. 1990 Clean Air Act
c. Comparative advertising
d. 33 Strategies of War

17. In statistics, _____ refers to techniques for the modeling and analysis of numerical data consisting of values of a dependent variable and of one or more independent variables The dependent variable in the regression equation is modeled as a function of the independent variables, corresponding parameters, and an error term. The error term is treated as a random variable and represents unexplained variation in the dependent variable.
a. Regression analysis
b. Stepwise regression
c. Trend analysis
d. Least squares

18. The _____ is a trilateral trade bloc in North America created by the governments of the United States, Canada, and Mexico. The agreement creating the trade bloc came into force on January 1, 1994. It superseded the Canada-United States Free Trade Agreement between the U.S. and Canada.
a. North American Free Trade Agreement
b. Business war game
c. Career portfolios
d. Trade union

19. _____ is an overall management philosophy introduced by Dr. Eliyahu M. Goldratt in his 1984 book titled The Goal, that is geared to help organizations continually achieve their goal. The title comes from the contention that any manageable system is limited in achieving more of its goal by a very small number of constraints, and that there is always at least one constraint. The _____ process seeks to identify the constraint and restructure the rest of the organization around it, through the use of the Five Focusing Steps.
   a. Six Sigma
   b. Production line
   c. Theory of constraints
   d. Takt time

Chapter 16. Scheduling

1. In probability theory, a probability distribution is called _____ if its cumulative distribution function is _____. This is equivalent to saying that for random variables X with the distribution in question, Pr[X = a] = 0 for all real numbers a, i.e.: the probability that X attains the value a is zero, for any number a. If the distribution of X is _____ then X is called a _____ random variable.
   a. Pay Band
   b. Connectionist expert systems
   c. Decision tree pruning
   d. Continuous

2. _____ is an overall management philosophy introduced by Dr. Eliyahu M. Goldratt in his 1984 book titled The Goal, that is geared to help organizations continually achieve their goal. The title comes from the contention that any manageable system is limited in achieving more of its goal by a very small number of constraints, and that there is always at least one constraint. The _____ process seeks to identify the constraint and restructure the rest of the organization around it, through the use of the Five Focusing Steps.
   a. Production line
   b. Six Sigma
   c. Takt time
   d. Theory of constraints

3. An _____ is a manufacturing process in which parts (usually interchangeable parts) are added to a product in a sequential manner using optimally planned logistics to create a finished product much faster than with handcrafting-type methods. The _____ developed by Ford Motor Company between 1908 and 1915 made _____s famous in the following decade through the social ramifications of mass production, such as the affordability of the Ford Model T and the introduction of high wages for Ford workers. However, the various preconditions for the development at Ford stretched far back into the 19th century, from the gradual realization of the dream of interchangeability, to the concept of reinventing workflow and job descriptions using analytical methods.
   a. Assembly line
   b. A4e
   c. A Stake in the Outcome
   d. AAAI

4. A _____ system is a manufacturing system in which there is some amount of flexibility that allows the system to react in the case of changes, whether predicted or unpredicted. This flexibility is generally considered to fall into two categories, which both contain numerous subcategories.

The first category, machine flexibility, covers the system's ability to be changed to produce new product types, and ability to change the order of operations executed on a part. The second category is called routing flexibility, which consists of the ability to use multiple machines to perform the same operation on a part, as well as the system's ability to absorb large-scale changes, such as in volume, capacity, or capability.

Chapter 16. Scheduling

a. Homeworkers
b. Manufacturing resource planning
c. Jidoka
d. Flexible manufacturing

5. _____ of the learning curve effect and the closely related experience curve effect express the relationship between equations for experience and efficiency or between efficiency gains and investment in the effort. The experience of 'learning curves' was first observed by the 19th Century German psychologist Hermann Ebbinghaus according to the difficulty of memorizing varying numbers of verbal stimuli, and subsequent learning about the complex processes of learning are discussed in the

.

The rule used for representing the learning curve effect states that the more times a task has been performed, the less time will be required on each subsequent iteration.

a. Distribution
b. Spatial Decision Support Systems
c. Point biserial correlation coefficient
d. Models

6. _____ ('Plan-Do-Check-Act') is an iterative four-step problem-solving process typically used in business process improvement. It is also known as the Deming Cycle, Shewhart cycle, Deming Wheel, or Plan-Do-Study-Act.

_____ was made popular by Dr. W. Edwards Deming, who is considered by many to be the father of modern quality control; however it was always referred to by him as the Shewhart cycle. Later in Deming's career, he modified _____ to Plan, Do, Study, Act (PDSA) so as to better describe his recommendations.

a. Management team
b. Management by exception
c. Decentralization
d. PDCA

7. _____ are statistical methods developed by Genichi Taguchi to improve the quality of manufactured goods, and more recently also applied to biotechnology, marketing and advertising. Professional statisticians have welcomed the goals and improvements brought about by _____, particularly by Taguchi's development of designs for studying variation, but have criticized the inefficiency of some of Taguchi's proposals.

Taguchi's work includes three principal contributions to statistics:

1. Taguchi loss function;
2. The philosophy of off-line quality control; and
3. Innovations in the design of experiments.

Traditionally, statistical methods have relied on mean-unbiased estimators of treatment effects: Under the conditions of the Gauss-Markov theorem, least squares estimators have minimum variance among all mean-unbiased estimators. The emphasis on comparisons of means also draws (limiting) comfort from the law of large numbers, according to which the sample means converge to the true mean.

 a. 28-hour day
 b. 1990 Clean Air Act
 c. Design of experiments
 d. Taguchi methods

8. _____ are typically small manufacturing operations that handle specialized manufacturing processes such as small customer orders or small batch jobs. _____ typically move on to different jobs (possibly with different customers) when each job is completed. By nature of this type of manufacturing operation, _____ are usually specialized in skill and processes.
 a. 1990 Clean Air Act
 b. 28-hour day
 c. 33 Strategies of War
 d. Job shops

9. _____ is a concept that aims to enhance supply chain integration by supporting and assisting joint practices. _____ seeks cooperative management of inventory through joint visibility and replenishment of products throughout the supply chain. Information shared between suppliers and retailers aids in planning and satisfying customer demands through a supportive system of shared information.
 a. Career portfolios
 b. Collaborative Planning, Forecasting and Replenishment
 c. Timesheets
 d. Groups decision making

10. _____ is a method of planning and managing projects that puts the main emphasis on the resources required to execute project tasks. It was developed by Eliyahu M. Goldratt. This is in contrast to the more traditional Critical Path and PERT methods, which emphasize task order and rigid scheduling. A Critical Chain project network will tend to keep the resources levelly loaded, but will require them to be flexible in their start times and to quickly switch between tasks and task chains to keep the whole project on schedule.

Chapter 16. Scheduling

a. Critical Chain Project Management
b. Project management office
c. Project engineer
d. Precedence diagram

11. _____ is a service policy where by the requests of customers or clients are attended to in the order that they arrived, without other biases or preferences. The policy can be employed when processing sales orders, in determining restaurant seating, or on a taxi stand, for example.

Festival seating (also known as general seating and stadium seating) is seating done on a FCFS basis.

a. 33 Strategies of War
b. 1990 Clean Air Act
c. First-come, first-served
d. 28-hour day

12. In economics, business, retail, and accounting, a _____ is the value of money that has been used up to produce something, and hence is not available for use anymore. In economics, a _____ is an alternative that is given up as a result of a decision. In business, the _____ may be one of acquisition, in which case the amount of money expended to acquire it is counted as _____.

a. Cost allocation
b. Cost
c. Cost overrun
d. Fixed costs

13. Business-to-consumer describes activities of businesses serving end consumers with products and/or services.

An example of a _____ transaction would be a person buying a pair of shoes from a retailer. The transactions that led to the shoes being available for purchase, that is the purchase of the leather, laces, rubber, etc.

a. B2C
b. PEST analysis
c. Market environment
d. Green marketing

Chapter 16. Scheduling

14. A _____ is a type of bar chart that illustrates a project schedule. _____s illustrate the start and finish dates of the terminal elements and summary elements of a project. Terminal elements and summary elements comprise the work breakdown structure of the project.

    a. 33 Strategies of War
    b. 1990 Clean Air Act
    c. Gantt chart
    d. 28-hour day

15. The _____ is a systematic, interactive forecasting method which relies on a panel of independent experts. The carefully selected experts answer questionnaires in two or more rounds. After each round, a facilitator provides an anonymous summary of the experts' forecasts from the previous round as well as the reasons they provided for their judgments.

    a. Hoshin Kanri
    b. Learning organization
    c. Quality function deployment
    d. Delphi method

16. The _____, widely known as ISO , is an international-standard-setting body composed of representatives from various national standards organizations. Founded on 23 February 1947, the organization promulgates worldwide proprietary industrial and commercial standards. It is headquartered in Geneva, Switzerland.

    a. A Stake in the Outcome
    b. International Organization for Standardization
    c. A4e
    d. AAAI

17. In economics, _____ is the desire to own something and the ability to pay for it. The term _____ signifies the ability or the willingness to buy a particular commodity at a given point of time.

    a. 33 Strategies of War
    b. 1990 Clean Air Act
    c. 28-hour day
    d. Demand

18. The metastability in flip-flops can be avoided by ensuring that the data and control inputs are held valid and constant for specified periods before and after the clock pulse, called the _____ and the hold time (t_h) respectively. These times are specified in the data sheet for the device, and are typically between a few nanoseconds and a few hundred picoseconds for modern devices.

Unfortunately, it is not always possible to meet the setup and hold criteria, because the flip-flop may be connected to a real-time signal that could change at any time, outside the control of the designer.

a. Setup time
b. 1990 Clean Air Act
c. 33 Strategies of War
d. 28-hour day

19. The _____ of 1938 (_____, ch. 676, 52 Stat. 1060, June 25, 1938, 29 U.S.C. ch.8), also called the Wages and Hours Bill, is United States federal law that applies to employees engaged in interstate commerce or employed by an enterprise engaged in commerce or in the production of goods for commerce, unless the employer can claim an exemption from coverage. The _____ established a national minimum wage, guaranteed time and a half for overtime in certain jobs, and prohibited most employment of minors in 'oppressive child labor,' a term defined in the statute.

a. Board of directors
b. Family and Medical Leave Act of 1993
c. Joint venture
d. Fair Labor Standards Act

20. _____ are conventions, treaties and recommendations designed to eliminate unjust and inhumane labour practices. The primary inernational agency charged with developing such standards is the International Labour Organization (ILO.) Established in 1919, the ILO advocates international standards as essential for the eradication of labour conditions involving 'injustice, hardship and privation'.

a. Airbus Industrie
b. Airbus SAS
c. Anaconda Copper
d. International labour standards

21. _____ is the body of laws, administrative rulings, and precedents which address the legal rights of, and restrictions on, working people and their organizations. As such, it mediates many aspects of the relationship between trade unions, employers and employees. In Canada, employment laws related to unionized workplaces are differentiated from those relating to particular individuals.

a. Shift work
b. Labor law
c. Trade union
d. Four-day week

22. _____ is an advertisement in which a particular product specifically mentions a competitor by name for the express purpose of showing why the competitor is inferior to the product naming it.

This should not be confused with parody advertisements, where a fictional product is being advertised for the purpose of poking fun at the particular advertisement, nor should it be confused with the use of a coined brand name for the purpose of comparing the product without actually naming an actual competitor. ('Wikipedia tastes better and is less filling than the Encyclopedia Galactica.')

In the 1980s, during what has been referred to as the cola wars, soft-drink manufacturer Pepsi ran a series of advertisements where people, caught on hidden camera, in a blind taste test, chose Pepsi over rival Coca-Cola.

a. 28-hour day
b. Comparative advertising
c. 1990 Clean Air Act
d. 33 Strategies of War

23. The _____ is the labour pool in employment. It is generally used to describe those working for a single company or industry, but can also apply to a geographic region like a city, country, state, etc. The term generally excludes the employers or management, and implies those involved in manual labour.
a. Work-life balance
b. Division of labour
c. Workforce
d. Pink-collar worker

Chapter 17. Project Management

1. _____ refers to the movement of cash into or out of a business or financial product. It is usually measured during a specified, finite period of time. Measurement of _____ can be used

- to determine a project's rate of return or value. The time of _____s into and out of projects are used as inputs in financial models such as internal rate of return, and net present value.
- to determine problems with a business's liquidity. Being profitable does not necessarily mean being liquid. A company can fail because of a shortage of cash, even while profitable.
- as an alternate measure of a business's profits when it is believed that accrual accounting concepts do not represent economic realities. For example, a company may be notionally profitable but generating little operational cash (as may be the case for a company that barters its products rather than selling for cash.) In such a case, the company may be deriving additional operating cash by issuing shares evaluating default risk, re-investment requirements, etc.

_____ is a generic term used differently depending on the context. It may be defined by users for their own purposes.

a. Sweat equity
b. Gross profit margin
c. Gross profit
d. Cash flow

2. _____ is the discipline of planning, organizing and managing resources to bring about the successful completion of specific project goals and objectives. It is often closely related to and sometimes conflated with Program management.

A project is a finite endeavor--having specific start and completion dates--undertaken to meet particular goals and objectives, usually to bring about beneficial change or added value.

a. Project engineer
b. Precedence diagram
c. Project management
d. Work package

3. _____ is a method of planning and managing projects that puts the main emphasis on the resources required to execute project tasks. It was developed by Eliyahu M. Goldratt. This is in contrast to the more traditional Critical Path and PERT methods, which emphasize task order and rigid scheduling. A Critical Chain project network will tend to keep the resources levelly loaded, but will require them to be flexible in their start times and to quickly switch between tasks and task chains to keep the whole project on schedule.
a. Project engineer
b. Critical Chain Project Management
c. Project management office
d. Precedence diagram

Chapter 17. Project Management

4. A _____ is a type of bar chart that illustrates a project schedule. _____s illustrate the start and finish dates of the terminal elements and summary elements of a project. Terminal elements and summary elements comprise the work breakdown structure of the project.
   a. 33 Strategies of War
   b. Gantt chart
   c. 1990 Clean Air Act
   d. 28-hour day

5. The _____, widely known as ISO , is an international-standard-setting body composed of representatives from various national standards organizations. Founded on 23 February 1947, the organization promulgates worldwide proprietary industrial and commercial standards. It is headquartered in Geneva, Switzerland.
   a. International Organization for Standardization
   b. A Stake in the Outcome
   c. A4e
   d. AAAI

6. The Program (or Project) Evaluation and Review Technique, commonly abbreviated _____, is a model for project management designed to analyze and represent the tasks involved in completing a given project.

   _____ is a method to analyze the involved tasks in completing a given project, specially the time needed to complete each task, and identifying the minimum time needed to complete the total project.

   _____ was developed primarily to simplify the planning and scheduling of large and complex projects.

   a. 1990 Clean Air Act
   b. 33 Strategies of War
   c. PERT
   d. 28-hour day

7. The _____, is a mathematically based algorithm for scheduling a set of project activities. It is an important tool for effective project management.

   It was developed in the 1950s by the Dupont Corporation at about the same time that General Dynamics and the US Navy were developing the Program Evaluation and Review Technique (PERT) Today, it is commonly used with all forms of projects, including construction, software development, research projects, product development, engineering, and plant maintenance, among others.

Chapter 17. Project Management

a. 33 Strategies of War
b. 1990 Clean Air Act
c. 28-hour day
d. Critical path method

8. _____ is a way of expressing knowledge or belief that an event will occur or has occurred. In mathematics the concept has been given an exact meaning in _____ theory, that is used extensively in such areas of study as mathematics, statistics, finance, gambling, science, and philosophy to draw conclusions about the likelihood of potential events and the underlying mechanics of complex systems.

The word _____ does not have a consistent direct definition.

a. Standard deviation
b. Probability
c. Time series analysis
d. Statistics

9. In statistics, _____ refers to techniques for the modeling and analysis of numerical data consisting of values of a dependent variable and of one or more independent variables The dependent variable in the regression equation is modeled as a function of the independent variables, corresponding parameters, and an error term. The error term is treated as a random variable and represents unexplained variation in the dependent variable.

a. Regression analysis
b. Trend analysis
c. Least squares
d. Stepwise regression

10. _____ is an advertisement in which a particular product specifically mentions a competitor by name for the express purpose of showing why the competitor is inferior to the product naming it.

This should not be confused with parody advertisements, where a fictional product is being advertised for the purpose of poking fun at the particular advertisement, nor should it be confused with the use of a coined brand name for the purpose of comparing the product without actually naming an actual competitor. ('Wikipedia tastes better and is less filling than the Encyclopedia Galactica.')

In the 1980s, during what has been referred to as the cola wars, soft-drink manufacturer Pepsi ran a series of advertisements where people, caught on hidden camera, in a blind taste test, chose Pepsi over rival Coca-Cola.

a. Comparative advertising
b. 1990 Clean Air Act
c. 33 Strategies of War
d. 28-hour day

11. _____ is a concept that aims to enhance supply chain integration by supporting and assisting joint practices. _____ seeks cooperative management of inventory through joint visibility and replenishment of products throughout the supply chain. Information shared between suppliers and retailers aids in planning and satisfying customer demands through a supportive system of shared information.
    a. Timesheets
    b. Career portfolios
    c. Groups decision making
    d. Collaborative Planning, Forecasting and Replenishment

12. The _____ is the labour pool in employment. It is generally used to describe those working for a single company or industry, but can also apply to a geographic region like a city, country, state, etc. The term generally excludes the employers or management, and implies those involved in manual labour.
    a. Work-life balance
    b. Division of labour
    c. Pink-collar worker
    d. Workforce

13. The _____ is a trilateral trade bloc in North America created by the governments of the United States, Canada, and Mexico. The agreement creating the trade bloc came into force on January 1, 1994. It superseded the Canada-United States Free Trade Agreement between the U.S. and Canada.
    a. North American Free Trade Agreement
    b. Trade union
    c. Career portfolios
    d. Business war game

ANSWER KEY

Chapter 1
1. d 2. a 3. c 4. c 5. d 6. d 7. c 8. b 9. c 10. d
11. d 12. c 13. c 14. b 15. b 16. b 17. d 18. d 19. a 20. c
21. d 22. a 23. d 24. d

Chapter 2
1. d 2. d 3. a 4. d 5. b 6. d 7. a 8. d 9. b 10. d
11. d 12. d 13. c 14. d 15. d 16. d 17. d 18. d 19. d 20. b
21. d 22. c 23. d 24. a 25. b 26. b 27. a 28. d 29. c 30. a
31. d

Chapter 3
1. d 2. b 3. d 4. b 5. d 6. c 7. d 8. d 9. d 10. b
11. b 12. d 13. c 14. a 15. d 16. d 17. a 18. b 19. b 20. c

Chapter 4
1. d 2. d 3. c 4. d 5. c 6. d 7. b 8. d 9. c 10. b
11. d 12. d 13. d 14. b 15. b 16. d 17. d 18. c 19. d 20. a
21. a 22. d 23. d 24. b

Chapter 5
1. d 2. d 3. d 4. b 5. d 6. a 7. b 8. a 9. d 10. d
11. d 12. a 13. c 14. d 15. c 16. a 17. c 18. c 19. d 20. d
21. d 22. d 23. d 24. b 25. b 26. d 27. d 28. b 29. b 30. d
31. d 32. d 33. d 34. c 35. d 36. d 37. b

Chapter 6
1. a 2. d 3. d 4. d 5. a 6. d 7. d 8. c 9. d 10. a
11. b 12. b 13. d 14. c 15. d 16. d 17. b 18. d 19. d

Chapter 7
1. c 2. a 3. d 4. b 5. c 6. a 7. a 8. d 9. d 10. d
11. c 12. b 13. d 14. d 15. c 16. d 17. a 18. d 19. d 20. a
21. d

Chapter 8
1. a 2. d 3. a 4. c 5. d 6. a 7. d 8. b 9. b 10. d
11. a 12. d 13. d 14. d 15. b 16. c 17. d 18. b 19. b 20. c
21. d 22. a 23. b 24. d

Chapter 9
1. a 2. c 3. b 4. d 5. c 6. d 7. b 8. d 9. b 10. c
11. d 12. b 13. c

Chapter 10
1. d   2. b   3. d   4. c   5. b   6. d   7. b   8. d   9. c   10. d
11. c   12. b

Chapter 11
1. d   2. d   3. d   4. d   5. a   6. d   7. d   8. d   9. c   10. c
11. d   12. d   13. c   14. d   15. d   16. a   17. b   18. d   19. a   20. b

Chapter 12
1. d   2. d   3. d   4. d   5. d   6. a   7. b   8. d   9. c   10. d
11. a   12. c   13. d   14. b   15. d   16. d   17. d

Chapter 13
1. d   2. c   3. a   4. d   5. d   6. d   7. b   8. b   9. a   10. d
11. c   12. d   13. d   14. a   15. d   16. b   17. c   18. d   19. c   20. d
21. a   22. a   23. d

Chapter 14
1. d   2. a   3. d   4. d   5. b   6. d   7. c   8. d   9. d   10. d
11. b   12. d   13. a   14. c   15. d   16. a

Chapter 15
1. a   2. a   3. d   4. d   5. a   6. d   7. a   8. b   9. d   10. d
11. c   12. d   13. d   14. a   15. c   16. c   17. a   18. a   19. c

Chapter 16
1. d   2. d   3. a   4. d   5. d   6. d   7. d   8. d   9. b   10. a
11. c   12. b   13. a   14. c   15. d   16. b   17. d   18. a   19. d   20. d
21. b   22. b   23. c

Chapter 17
1. d   2. c   3. b   4. b   5. a   6. c   7. d   8. b   9. a   10. a
11. d   12. d   13. a

www.ingramcontent.com/pod-product-compliance
Lightning Source LLC
Chambersburg PA
CBHW082047230426
43670CB00016B/2811